ISLAM AND MUSLIM CIVILIZATION

A Supplementary Social Studies Unit for Grade Six

Written by Susan Douglass
Illustrated by Abd Al-Muttalib Fahemy

Goodword**kidz**
Helping you build a family of faith

First published 1995 by
The International Institute of Islamic Thought (IIIT)
500 Grove St., 2nd Floor
Herndon, VA 20170-4735, USA
Tel: (1-703) 471 1133 / Fax: (1-703) 471 3922
E-mail: iiit@iiit.org / URL: http://www.iiit.org

First published by Goodword Books in 2003
Reprinted 2004
in arrangement with The International Institute of Islamic Thought
© The International Institute of Islamic Thought 1995

Goodword Books Pvt. Ltd.
1, Nizamuddin West Market
New Delhi 110 013
e-mail: info@goodwordbooks.com
Printed in India

www.goodwordbooks.com

IIIT is a cultural and intellectual foundation registered in the United States of America in 1981 with the objectives of providing a comprehensive Islamic outlook through elucidating the principle of Islam and relating them to relevant issues of contemporary thought: regaining the intellectual, cultural, and civilizational identity of the ummah through Islamization of the various disciplines of knowledge, to rectify the methodology of contemporary Islamic thought in order to enable it to resume its contribution to the progress of human civilization and give it meaning and direction in line with the values and objectives of Islam.

IIIT seeks to achieve its objectives by holding specialized academic seminars and conferences, supporting educational and cultural institutions and projects, supporting and guiding graduate and post-graduate studies.

The IIIT Islamic School Book Project supports the writing, publication, and distribution of books and other teaching material for schools as part of its effort to present the true picture of Islam in a factual objective way. These educational resources, developed under the general guidelines of the IIIT Islamization of Knowledge program, cover the following fields: Islamic Studies, Social Studies, Literature, Science and Mathematics. International collaboration and coordination with teachers, schools and organizations is assured through the International Forum for Education Resources for Islamic English-medium schools.

For more information contact:

The Director
IIIT Islamic School Book Project
International Institute of Islamic Thought (IIIT)
500 Grove St., 2nd Floor,
Herndon, VA 20170-4735, USA
Tel: (1-703) 471 1133 / Fax: (1-703) 471 3922
E-mail: iiit@iiit.org / URL: http://www.iiit.org

ABOUT THE AUTHOR

Susan Douglass is an American-born Muslim who accepted Islam in 1974. She received the Bachelor of Arts in History from the University of Rochester in 1972. She received the Master of Arts in Arab Studies from Georgetown University in 1992. She holds teaching certification in social studies from New York and Virginia.

She has taught in a variety of settings and subjects, beginning with volunteer work in Headstart in 1965. She taught and coordinated art classes in a summer youth program from 1970-72 in Rochester, NY. Since returning to the U.S. in 1984, from extended stays in Germany and Egypt, she resumed work in education. She has taught arts, crafts and story sessions in Muslim summer school programs for several years in Herndon, VA. As teacher and Head of the Social Studies Department at the Islamic Saudi Academy, Fairfax, VA, she taught both elementary and secondary social studies, built a supplementary resource library, and led in preparing a K-12 social studies curriculum utilizing both American and Arab resources for the Academy's accreditation. The current IIIT project was conceived and developed in the classroom. The author is involved in numerous other educational projects, including work as reviewer and consultant to major textbook publishers in the field of social studies. She has reviewed and offered revisions to the California History/Social Science Framework (1994) and the National History Standards Project (1994), in addition to various projects for the Council on Islamic Education in Fountain Valley, CA, including a book, *Strategies and Structures for Presenting World History, with Islam and Muslim History as a Case Study* (Council on Islamic Education, 1994.)

ADVISORY PANEL MEMBERS

Rahima Abdullah
Elementary Coordinator
Islamic Saudi Academy, Alexandria, VA

Dr. Kadija A. Ali
Educational Projects Coordinator
International Institute of Islamic Thought,
Herndon, VA

Jinan N. Alkhateeb
Social Studies Teacher
Islamic Saudi Academy, Alexandria, VA

Mrs. Hamida Amanat
Director of Education
American Islamic Academy
Curriculum Consultant
Al-Ghazaly School, Pine brook, NJ

Shaker El Sayed
Coordinator
Islamic Teaching Center, Islamic Schools
Department
Islamic Society of North America, Plainfield,
IN

Dr. Tasneema Ghazi
IQRA International Educational Foundation,
Chicago, IL

Dr. Zakiyyah Muhammad
Universal Institute of Islamic Education,
Sacramento, CA

ACKNOWLEDGEMENTS

Many people's efforts have contributed to producing this series of supplementary units for Social Studies. First, I am grateful to the International Institute of Islamic Thought (IIIT) for placing their confidence in me to undertake a project of this size and for providing all the financial and logistical resources needed for its completion. I would like to thank Dr. Mahmud Rashdan, under whose guidance this project began in 1988. His wisdom helped to set it on a solid foundation. Without constant support and encouragement by Dr. Omar Kasule, project director 1991-present, and Dr. Khadija Ali Sharief, project coordinator (1993-present), this unit would never have met the light of day.

The project has been much enhanced by the members of the Advisory Panel. In addition to offering guidance on the project as a whole, they have spent much time and detailed effort on each individual manuscript. These brothers and sisters are all active education professionals with a broad range of experience and a long list of accomplishments.

May Allah reward my family and grant them patience for sacrificing some degree of comfort so that I, as wife and mother, might realize this goal. I owe special thanks to my husband, Usama Amer, for his constant help with the computer, with Arabic sources and many other matters of consultation. With regard to the writing and editing process, I thank my students at the Islamic Saudi Academy who fired my enthusiam for research and writing, and who used this unit in the raw material stage. I thank the teachers and students at ISA and elsewhere who have used the manuscript for this unit in their classes and helped me to refine the material. Among the panel member/teachers who have done so are Rahima Abdullah and Jinan Al-Khateeb. Many others have offered suggestions, including Dr. Freda Shamma and Dr. Anwar Hajjaj. Gratitude is extended to Rabiah Abdullah, whose keen mind and sharp pencil have shaped and pruned text for the whole project, and who also used this unit in her classes.

It has been a pleasure to work on several units with the illustrator, Abd al-Muttalib Fahemy, who contributed his skill and dedication, bringing enthusiasm and a rare willingness to go the extra mile to research a sketch or detail for accuracy. Finally, thanks to the many people at Kendall/Hunt Publishing Co. who graciously met my many requests and turned tentative, complex and unfamiliar material into a finished product.

May Allah reward the efforts of sincere workers, especially the teachers and students for whom this unit was written.

Susan Douglass
Falls Church, Virginia
September 1994

5

TABLE OF CONTENTS

Part I: Teacher's Notes

Introduction 8

Purpose and Placement 8

A Note on the Use of Terminology 9

Unit Overview 10

Conceptual Outline 11

Unit Objectives 16

Part II: Student Text, Chapter One "The Coming of Islam"

Section 1 24

Section 2 28

Section 3 32

Section 4 38

Part III: Student Text, Chapter Two "Muslim Civilization"

Section 1 50

Section 2 57

Section 3 67

Section 4 77

Words to Remember 82

Part IV: Teaching Suggestions and Enrichment Activities

Lessons, Chapter One 84

Lessons, Chapter Two 87

Bibliography 92

Comprehension Questions – Key 94

Part V: Unit Activities

Worksheets 103

Test Question File 112

Part I:

Teacher's Notes

INTRODUCTION

This unit is the seventh in a series of supplementary units for the social studies, grades K-12. The series is an effort to offer an accurate and critical treatment of Islam in those areas of the curriculum which deal with it directly, and to introduce it into areas where an understanding of the role of Muslims is an essential part of events. The series is motivated by the belief that "history" should be remembered because it makes sense and it is enjoyable, and that even young students should be introduced to skills and concepts of historical scholarship.

An important requirement in the design of this supplementary series is that each unit feature skills and concepts typical for the scope and sequence of the social studies curriculum in its grade level. Topics are similarly chosen for their close relationship to typical courses offered at or near their grade level. The units are intended to fulfill the classroom teacher's need for curriculum materials reflecting a high level of historical scholarship and student interest without long hours of teacher research and preparation.

PURPOSE AND PLACEMENT OF THE UNIT

This unit is intended to provide upper elementary and junior high school students with an introduction to Islam and the civilization which Muslims built.

The scope of the materials offered here make it possible to substitute them for typical textbook units on Islam and Muslims, which are generally inadequate and faulty in many ways. The guiding objective of this unit is that the students acquire basic familiarity with Islam's major tenets and the progress and contributions of Muslims who carried Islam onto the world stage. Its essential objective is to provide historical context to the emergence of Islam, and to deal with a broad range of historical issues surrounding the rise of Islam in an intellectually satisfying manner, by citing historical evidence.

Chronologically accurate placement of the unit is following the fall of the Western Roman Empire and its continuation as Byzantium. By placing units on Islamic, African and East Asian civilizations in random sequence, textbook treatments of world history often fail to show that civilizations outside of Europe contributed to gradual and interdependent global development toward the modern world. Civilizations of China, India, Africa and the Near East are fixed in students' minds as "also-rans" of history.

Current historical scholarship recognizes that Europe's Renaissance and later dominance would have been unthinkable without direct cross-pollination from other parts of the Old World. Over a period of more than a thousand years, Muslim rulers were a major factor in the political equation of the Old World. Islamic civilization was a crucible of technological and scientific knowledge from the known world up to its time. In trade, it formed a hinge between East and West. New studies are still uncovering evidence of influence on Europe from Muslim and other non-Western sources.

The terms "Islam" and "Muslim" are not interchangeable, and are often misused. In this unit, "Islam" refers to the set of religious beliefs and attitudes encompassed by the *Qur'an* and the example of Muhammad ﷺ. "Muslim" refers to the followers of Islam, and is used here as an adjective referring to social, cultural, political or economic institutions built by followers of Islam. In the literal sense, "Muslim" means a person who is at peace with Allah, or God, through obedience and submission to Him. Judgment on whether a person is Muslim rests with Allah alone. For a follower of Islam, it is a challenge and an aspiration.

The reason for not using the term "Islamic" to refer to institutions built by "Muslims" is that they have not always measured up to Islamic standards and ideals. This use of the terms is not entirely satisfactory, but they were chosen for the sake of simplicity. In his excellent and thorough study, *The Venture of Islam: History and Conscience in a World Civilization*, Marshall G.S. Hodgson uses the terms "Islamic" and "Islamicate" to make the same distinction more satisfactorily.

The confusion of terms has led to major misunderstandings by historians and students. For example, we have many books on "Islamic Art," in which some of the pieces shown contradict Islamic principles of non-representation of animate creatures. More important, the confusion of terms has led to condemnation of Islam itself for the mistakes of its fallible human followers. We strive to avoid this difficulty in the present introduction to Islam and Muslim civilization for young students.

This unit is prepared as an introduction to Islamic civilization for upper elementary and junior high school students. It may be used as a supplement to world history, civilizations, or world cultures studies at that level.

Chapter One begins by placing Arabia in historical context. Tracing the story of the caravans, the patriarch Abraham, and the city of Makkah, a brief account of Muhammad's ﷺ early life is given. Muhammad's prophethood is divided into two periods — 10 years of teaching in Makkah, and 13 years from the migration (Hijra) to Medina to his death in 632 C.E. Major tenets of Islam relevant to the individual Muslim and the community are described. The progress of Islam from persecution in Makkah to acceptance in the whole Arabian Peninsula is traced.

Chapter Two is a survey of the civilization built by Muslims as they tried to live up to the challenge of their Islamic beliefs and responsibilities. It is divided into four sections, each of which covers one aspect of Muslim activity.

- **Section 1** covers the expansion of Islam beyond the borders of the Arabian Peninsula. Major events, causes and means of expansion are summarized.

- **Section 2** focuses on the challenge of governing the lands by Islam. The problems faced by Muslims in ruling such vast and diverse lands are outlined. A brief chronological summary of ruling groups is provided together with discussion of their contributions.

- **Section 3** describes the preservation and spread of knowledge about Islam. It describes the development of the branches of religious sciences. It explains the efforts of legal scholars to establish consensus on the body of Islamic law, and to make Muslim rulers accountable. Technological and scientific accomplishments of Muslims from the 7th to the 16th centuries are cited. The section concludes with a discussion of cultural and scientific influence upon European civilization.

- **Section 4** illustrates 14th century Muslim urban culture by taking the student along on part of the famous 14th century traveler Ibn Battuta's journey.

Other features of the unit combine to give the students a solid impression of Islamic civilization. Accompanying Chapter Two, a videotape reinforces, illustrates and enriches material presented briefly in the text. The tape includes information on the spread of Islam, Islamic scientific activity, and the influence of Islamic culture in Europe. A set of worksheets reinforces concepts presented in the text and builds skill by encouraging students to work with and apply information. Maps are provided for orientation and explanation. Illustrations in the text are coloring book pages, which may be used for detailed picture study. Teaching suggestions, supplementary activities and a reference section are provided to guide discussion.

CHAPTER ONE:

Section 1:
1. The caravan route through Arabia was a source of important goods for the ancient world.
2. Cities developed along the caravan route when desert nomads settled and began to farm and trade.
3. Makkah, founded by patriarch Abraham, became important as a center of trade and place of religious pilgrimage.
4. Quraysh, the resident tribe in Makkah, became wealthy and powerful through trade and control of the Kaabah.

Section 2:
1. Muhammad ﷺ was born in 570 C.E. in Makkah, to the Quraysh tribe.
2. He was orphaned, lived with relatives, worked as a shepherd and travelled with his uncle's and Khadijah's caravans.
3. He was highly respected by his tribe for honesty and tact.
4. The wealthy widow Khadijah and Muhammad ﷺ married and had many children.

Section 3:
1. While he was staying in the cave at Hira', he received revelation from Allah.
2. The word for God in Arabic is **Allah**, **Islam** means submission to God, and a **Muslim** is one who submits to God's will.
3. Islam teaches that Muhammad ﷺ was the last prophet of many, including the prophets Ibrahim, Musa and Issa, among others.
4. Those who believed in Muhammad's prophethood and message were few at first, but gradually increased in number and strength.
5. The wealthy chiefs of Quraysh rejected Islam and persecuted the Muslims.
6. The Muslims did not give up their faith under persecution, and Quraysh failed to make Muhammad ﷺ stop teaching.
7. People from the city of Yathrib accepted Islam and offered protection to the Muslims of Makkah.
8. Muhammad ﷺ sent groups of migrants to Yathrib, Quraysh plotted to murder him, but he escaped to Yathrib.

Section 4:

1. Muhammad's migration, called Hijra, marks the beginning of the Muslim calendar.
2. Yathrib was renamed by the Muslims **Medinat Al-Nabi**, and it became home to the Muslim community.
3. Muhajirun ("migrants" from Makkah) were joined by Muhammad ﷺ in brotherhood with Ansar ("helpers" from Medina).
4. The first mosque was built and the call to prayer established.
5. The **Qur'an** was the message which Muhammad ﷺ received over a period of 23 years.
6. Muslims honor the **Qur'an** as revelation from Allah .
7. Rules for building personal and community life are contained in **Qur'an** and Muhammad's example.
8. Islamic rules became laws of the Muslim community at Medina.
9. Makkan Quraysh continued their efforts against the Muslims.
10. Muslims at Medina planned to resist Quraysh by disturbing their caravans.
11. Several battles ensued between Quraysh and its allies, and the Muslims and their allies.
12. The Muslims grew in strength and influence in Arabia.
13. A non-agression treaty was made with Quraysh; it was broken, and the Muslims entered Makkah in strength without fighting.
14. Islam was established in the Ka'aba, Quraysh became Muslim, and most Arabian tribes accepted Islam.
15. Muhammad ﷺ made a final pilgrimmage and farewell speech, and he died a short time later.
16. The Muslims and their leaders felt responsible for continuing Muhammad's work.

CHAPTER TWO:

Section 1:

1. Muslims built a civilization in their attempt to live up to Islamic standards and spread the faith.
2. **Jihad** means both "personal effort" and "fighting to defend Islam against persecution."
3. Freedom of religion did not exist long ago; people had to follow their government's religion or risk persecution.
4. Muslims fought to end persecution and guarantee religious freedom in order to spread Islam.
5. Islamic law introduced strict controls on fighting where none existed before.
6. The Persian and Byzantine Empires north of Arabia were weakened by fighting and discontented citizens.

7. Moving northeast and northwest, Muslim armies toppled both empires and established rule in the area from the Atlantic to China's borders by 750 C.E., or about 100 years after Hijra.
8. Muslims ruled in Spain for 700 years, until 1492.
9. Many people accepted Islam, while others continued to practice their beliefs in tolerance and safety.
10. Islam continued to spread slowly through the influential state, through learning and trade.
11. Islam is still spreading through the influence of migration and learning.

Section 2:
1. Early Muslim rulers faced problems of the lands' size (transport, communication) and diversity (geography, language, culture).
2. Muslims needed to establish just authority, representation and local government, laws, and structures to connect the lands.
3. The people's former experience made them expect royal government and behavior from the Muslim rulers.
4. The conflict between the challenge of ruling by Islamic ideals and the temptation of wealth and power created problems.
5. Arab Muslim government was accepted by people in the early state.
6. For 30 years, "Rightly-Guided **Khalifahs**" ruled selflessly and wisely according to Islamic principles.
7. After a period of difficulties **(fitnah)**, Umayyad rulers formed a dynasty and moved the capital to Damascus, from 661-750.
8. Umayyads were strong rulers and organizers, but abandoned some Islamic ideals.
9. Abbassids unseated Umayyads, established a new dynasty from 750-945, and moved the capital to Baghdad.
10. Umayyads set up a separate dynasty in Spain.
11. Baghdad became a center of administration, trade and high culture and learning.
12. Abbassid rulers advanced civilization in many areas, but they abandoned Islamic principles of simplicity for imperial styles of rule.
13. Seljuk Turks and other groups opposed the later Abbassids, and the Khalifal state broke up into many smaller states.
14. Lack of unity in the Muslim state led to invasions and loss of territory.
15. Central Asian Mongol tribes invaded Europe and Asia in the 1200s, causing destruction and building a huge empire.
16. The Mongol empire broke up, most accepted Islamic beliefs and culture, and established Muslim governments.
17. Ottoman Turks established control over large areas of the Muslim lands from the 1300s to the 20th century.
18. The Ottoman state contributed to advancements in culture and military organization.
19. Scholars seek to safeguard and implement Islamic principles through careful study of **Qur'an, Sunnah** and other legal sciences.

20.   Scholars establish **Shari'ah**, fundamental rules and standards for private and official behavior to unite Muslims and preserve Islamic ideals.

Section 3:

1.   The spread of knowledge in Islamic civilization began with careful preservation and teaching about Islam.
2.   The **Qur'an** is the most important source of knowledge about Islam, and Muslims made every effort to ensure its authenticity.
3.   Muhammad's **Sunnah**, or example, is preserved in books of **Hadith** as the second important source of Islamic knowledge.
4.   The spread of Islamic knowledge combined with the heritage of the Mediterranean, India and China to bring many advancements in science.
5.   Muslim rulers encouraged and financed much scientific and literary work.
6.   Muslim scientists were universal scholars who studied and wrote on many subjects.
7.   Muslim works on mathematics, medicine, astronomy and other subjects were used and respected for centuries in the West and elsewhere.
8.   Muslim learning spread among Muslim lands and on to Europe through trade, travel and the invention of paper books.
9.   Spain and Italy were important routes through which Muslim learning spread to Europe and brought **Rennaissance**. *(Note: This concept is merely introduced for later reference in the students' study of Europe.)*

Section 4:

1.   The Moroccan **Ibn Battuta** was a world traveller for about 30 years during the 14th century.
2.   Beginning with a pilgrimage to Makkah, he visited many lands and cities, travelling on foot, by caravan, oxcart, and ship.
3.   Bazaars supplied people in Muslim lands with necessities and luxuries from Asia, Africa and Europe.
4.   Cairo was a large city with many facilities for residents, travellers, students, merchants and traders.
5.   Damascus and Jerusalem were important cities in the Muslim lands.
6.   Makkah was a desert city far from other centers, but during the pilgrimage each year it came alive with people and goods from many lands.
7.   Islam encourages people of many races and nationalities to mingle freely and fulfill their religious duties side by side as equals.
8.   Baghdad was a trade hub where many land and sea routes converged.
9.   Muslim trade routes covered the Mediterranean, the Sahara, the Arabian Peninsula, parts of Asia including the Silk Road, the Indian Ocean basin, and from the Spice Islands to China on the Pacific.
10.   Many fruits and vegetables common in the West today were introduced by Muslim merchants.
11.   Muslim seamen used compasses and astrolabes to navigate by the stars at sea.

12. They sailed in triangular-sailed ships, using seasonal monsoon winds to trade across the Indian Ocean.
13. Parts of India were ruled by the Mughals at Delhi.
14. Malacca was an important port on the passage to the China Sea; Islam had already spread there by the 14th century.
15. Muslim scholars, judges and other religious men and merchants were an international class at home in many lands.
16. The African Sahara contained important Muslim cities and trade routes which supplied two-thirds of the Europe's gold in the 14th century.
17. Ibn Battuta dictated the story of his travels, called the *Rihlah*.

MAP SKILLS: The student will:

CHAPTER ONE:

- Describe the geographic setting of Arabia.
- Trace the ancient incense trade route from Yemen to Egypt and Rome.
- Locate the Arabian Peninsula, Red Sea and Mediterranean Sea.
- Locate Makkah and Medina (Yathrib).

CHAPTER TWO:

- Locate Syria, Palestine, and the Persian and Byzantine Empires.
- Trace the Nile River, Tigris-Euphrates River, Persian (Arabian) Gulf, Indian Ocean, Arabian Sea.
- Outline (and name major regions of) Muslim lands around 750 C.E. and 1460 C.E.
- Locate other major lands and cities mentioned in the text.
- Trace trade routes used by Muslim merchants around the 14th century and list important products.
- Describe the geographic setting of the Muslim lands.

CONTENT OBJECTIVES: The student will:

CHAPTER ONE:

- Describe caravan trade along the incense route in Arabia.
- Define nomad, oasis and describe the desert tribes' culture.
- Trace the development of Makkah and list reasons for itsimportance before and after Muhammad's prophethood.
- Describe the Arabs' religion before Islam and compare it with Islamic beliefs and practices.
- Describe the chronological outline of Muhammad's life and trace the progress. of the Muslim community from the beginning of Muhammad's mission to his death.
- Give the meaning of the following terms: Allah, Islam, Muslim, Qur'an, Hajj, Hijrah, Ka'aba, masjid (mosque).
- Name major groups and individuals who participated in the story of Islam.
- Define persecution and describe the conflict between Quraysh, Muhammad (pbuh), and the emerging Muslim community.
- Explain the significance of the **Qur'an** in Islam and outline important elements of belief and rules for community life.
- Explain the role of prophethood in Islam and the importance of Muhammad's example to Muslims.

CHAPTER TWO:

Section 1:
- Trace the spread of Islam in the first 100-200 years after Muhammad's death.
- List several ways in which Islam was spread.
- Define **jihad** and explain its significance in Islam.
- Describe the relation between religion and government long ago.
- List Islamic rules controlling warfare by armies and discuss application of these standards to past and present conflicts.
- Describe the role of trade in spreading Islam and locate areas into which Islam was spread through trade.

Section 2:
- List challenges faced by the early Muslim rulers after the rapid expansion.
- List elements of sound government over a large state.
- Explain the role of the original Arab Muslims in the new state.
- Name the "Rightly-Guided Khalifahs" and list characteristics of their rule.
- Discuss major political events in the progress of the Muslim state.
- Identify major ruling groups (Umayyad, Abbassid, Seljuk, Mongol[Mughal], Ottoman) and list characteristics of their rule.
- Compare characteristics of rule among the early community at Medina with that of later ruling groups.
- List major cultural achievments of each ruling group.
- List reasons for some Muslims' dissatisfaction with ruling groups and describe the action they took.
- Describe the work of Muslim scholars to establish Islamic standards for individuals and governments and its results beginning of Muhammad's mission to his death.
- Give the meaning of the following terms: Allah, Islam, Muslim, Qur'an, Hajj, Hijrah, Ka'aba, masjid (mosque).
- Name major groups and individuals who participated in the story of Islam.
- Define persecution and describe the conflict between Quraysh, Muhammad ﷺ and the emerging Muslim community.
- Explain the significance of the Qur'an in Islam and outline important elements of belief and rules for community life.
- Explain the role of prophethood in Islam and the importance of Muhammad's example to Muslims.

Section 3:
- Describe the efforts of Muslims to preserve **Qur'an** and **Sunnah**.
- Explain how study of Islamic knowledge led to other sciences.
- List previous civilizations whose accomplishments contributed to Muslim learning and science.

- Discuss the role of translations and transmission of knowledge between various civilizations and list ways in which contact occurs.
- Identify some important Muslim scientists, writers and scholars and list their achievements.
- Compare the characteristics of civilization and cultural achievements of the Muslims with those of other civilizations studied (Egypt, Greece, Rome, China, etc).
- Trace the spread of Muslim scholarship, inventions and trade to Europe before the Rennaissance.

Section 4:
- Identify Ibn Battuta and trace his itinerary on a map.
- Characterize the standard of living in major Muslim cities.
- Describe possibilities and conveniences for travel in Muslim lands during the 14th century.
- Describe Makkah during the pilgrimage and compare it to ancient Makkah before Muhammad ﷺ.
- List important trade goods which came from and through Muslim lands, trace trade routes and match them to forms of transport.
- List types of people who made up the class of international travelers in the Muslim lands and give reasons for their travel.
- Explain the significance of the mingling of Muslims from many lands, skin colors, cultures and religions and discuss probable outcomes and advantages.

ISLAM AND MUSLIM CIVILIZATION

CHAPTER ONE

"The Coming of Islam"

Written by Susan Douglass
Illustrated by Abd Al-Muttalib Fahemy and Susan Douglass

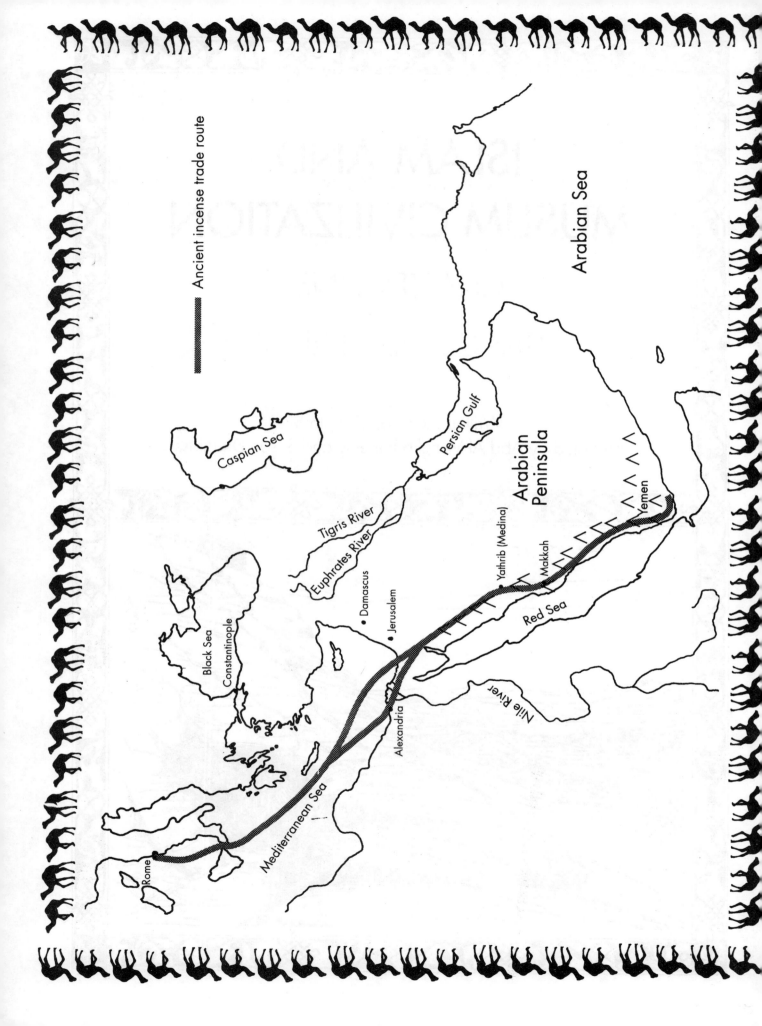

Ancient incense trade route

Arabian Sea

Caspian Sea

Arabian Peninsula

Persian Gulf

Tigris River

Euphrates River

Yemen

Yathrib (Medina)

Makkah

Red Sea

Damascus

Jerusalem

Black Sea

Constantinople

Nile River

Alexandria

Mediterranean Sea

Rome

The Coming of Islam

رَبَّنَآ إِنِّى أَسْكَنتُ مِن ذُرِّيَّتِى بِوَادٍ غَيْرِ ذِى زَرْعٍ عِندَ بَيْتِكَ
ٱلْمُحَرَّمِ رَبَّنَا لِيُقِيمُوا۟ ٱلصَّلَوٰةَ فَٱجْعَلْ أَفْـِٔدَةً مِّنَ ٱلنَّاسِ
تَهْوِىٓ إِلَيْهِمْ وَٱرْزُقْهُم مِّنَ ٱلثَّمَرَٰتِ لَعَلَّهُمْ يَشْكُرُونَ

O our Lord! I have made some of my offspring to dwell
In a valley without cultivation by Thy sacred house;
In order, our Lord, that they may establish regular prayer;
So fill the hearts of some among men with love towards them,
And feed them with fruits, so that they may give thanks.

(Qur'an, 14:37)

A cloud of smoke rises from an altar in the Roman temple. Speaking a prayer, the priest waves his hands through the smoke. He hopes the sweet smell of incense will bring an answer to his prayer. On the beach in a Roman harbor, slaves unload leather sacks. One of the sacks tears open, and clumps of yellow crystals fall onto the sand. The overseer shouts and snaps a whip. A slave tucks a piece of precious incense into his belt. In Alexandria, Egypt, cargo from canal boats is loaded into square-sailed Roman ships that will carry it across the Mediterranean. Slaves stow the leather sacks on deck along with glass, jewels and ivory bound for the rich capital of Rome.

Merchants bargain for the best price at a market along the canal. Dressed in wide robes, they wrap the loose end of their turbans across their faces to keep out the dust. Behind them, thin camels drink at the river and nibble grass. Their backs are free of wooden boxes, bundles of silk and cotton cloth, and sacks of frankincense. The caravan brought these loads across the mountains through Arabia from Yemen, far to the South. In Yemen, a Bedouin cuts a patch of bark from a desert tree. Later he returns to scrape off the golden crystals of dried sap. This precious stuff is burned as fragrant incense in temples all over the ancient world.

Part II:

Student Text

Chapter One

Arabia Before Muhammad

For more than a thousand years, caravans made their way along this important route. They brought incense for ancient Egyptian, Greek and Roman temples where priests led worship of their many gods. Along with the incense, they carried cloth, jewels and other goods from Asia and Africa. The caravans passed by ruins of towns and cities. There ancient prophets had preached belief in One God, and found few followers at first.

THE DESERT TRIBES

Caravans passed through the territory of desert **nomad** tribes. Tribesmen lived in the harsh land by moving constantly with their grazing animals among the scattered **oases**, or fertile spots with water. They had to be fiercely loyal to their families to survive, and often fought with other tribes. They were generous to guests and travelers in trouble. They knew that the hard desert makes people equal. They respected skill and courage. They loved the freedom of the wide sky and endless land. They sang about their life in long poems, which they could memorize after hearing only once! Their language—Arabic—was rich in describing things around them and expressing strong feelings.

CITIES ON THE TRADE ROUTE

At some **oases**, towns and small cities grew up where caravans stopped to rest and trade for supplies. Desert tribes settled down to farm. Where there was enough water, tribes grew date palms, grapes and grain. Caravans traded goods for these food supplies. Bedouins brought their animals to town, selling meat, milk and riding animals to city-dwellers and caravans. In their shops, craftsmen worked with wood, stone, leather and metal. They made things for beauty, travel and war. Merchants of the towns became rich. They sent great caravans across Arabia to trade in summer and winter.

THE STORY OF MAKKAH

The most important city on this route along the mountains was Makkah. The map on page 14 shows Makkah in a dry valley near the Red Sea. The city was founded long ago by Ibrahim, the father of the prophets. Allah ordered him to bring part of his family, his wife Hajar and their baby son Isma'il, to settle there. Searching for water, Hajar ran back and forth between the hills of Safa and Marwa. Then the well of Zamzam bubbled up when the Angel Jibril struck the earth with his heel. Mother and son settled there with people of the local tribes. Later, Ibrahim and his son Ismail, built a house for worship of Allah. It was a simple cube of stones with one door and a black stone at one corner. The house was called the Kaabah, meaning "cube."

People from the desert tribes came to visit this house and share in worship. Later generations brought **idols** (statues for worship) to the Kaabah. They worshipped spirits of war and rain, of sun and moon, trees and rocks. Only a few people called **Hunafa'** kept up the belief in One God.

The tradition of **pilgrimage**, or visiting the Kaabah, continued. Each year, tribes from all over Arabia came to Makkah to worship their idols. They sang, danced and made sacrifices. They competed in wealth and ceremonies, and Arabic poetry. The Makkan tribe had the honor of caring for the Kaabah. They provided food and water for the **pilgrims**. The celebration was also good business. Pilgrims bought and sold many things during their visit.

MAKKAH BECAME AN IMPORTANT CITY

Makkah had a good location, water supply and many visitors. The city grew into a caravan stop and trading center. The Makkans became rich and powerful. They were respected as keepers of the Kaabah.. Their caravans carried goods from Asia and Africa to the empires of Rome and Persia. Some cara-

Before Islam, the pilgrimmage at Makkah was a great festival for Arab tribes. Idols from many tribes were placed in and around the Ka'abah.

vans had thousands of loaded camels! Makkans made treaties with many tribes so that their caravans could travel safely. During certain **sacred** (holy) months, no tribe could attack another. Both caravans and pilgrims depended on the treaties for peace. The Makkans backed up their power with weapons and skills in war.

Understanding Section 1:

1. What important product was carried by caravans through Arabia in ancient times?

2. How did the desert tribes survive in the harsh land of Arabia? What personal qualities did they need?

3. For what purpose did Ibrahim build the Kaabah, and how did later generations change the Kaabah?

4. What caused Makkah to grow and become a city?

Muhammad's Life Before Prophethood

About 570 years after the birth of Jesus, Muhammad ﷺ was born into this Makkan tribe, called Quraysh. Even before Muhammad's birth, signs showed that this family enjoyed special favor with Allah. Muhammad's grandfather, Abd Al-Muttalib, followed a dream to rediscover the buried well of Zamzam. He also dug up some treasure left by the tribe who had buried it. Another famous story tells how Muhammad's father was nearly killed.

Abd Al-Muttalib had made a vow, or promise, to Allah that if he had ten sons who grew to be men, he would sacrifice one of them. Ten sons were born and all of them grew into fine young men. Abd Al-Muttalib kept his vow. He drew lots to find out which of his sons would be sacrificed. The draw fell on his favorite son Abdullah, the youngest. He told Abdullah and prepared to carry out his vow. When other members of the tribe heard about it, they tried to stop him. They loved Abdullah, and they did not want Abd Al-Muttalib to do something other chiefs might imitate. They looked for a way to save Abdullah without breaking the vow. They went to a wise, old woman to seek advice. She suggested a plan.

The ancient Arabs used to draw lots with arrows. Abd Al-Muttalib should take one arrow and mark it for Abdullah, and place it with another arrow that represented 10 camels. If the camels' arrow was drawn, he was to sacrifice the 10 camels and let Abdullah live. If the draw fell to Abdullah, the old woman told him to add 10 more camels. He did this, and each time the draw fell on Abdullah. Each time 10 more camels were added, until the number of camels had reached 100! Finally, the camels' arrow was drawn. To be sure, he repeated the draw three times. Three times the draw fell to the camels. A great sacrifice was held. The people rejoiced, and marveled at Abdullah's great worth in the sight of God. One hundred camels was a fortune in wealth.

Abdullah became the father of Muhammad ﷺ.

The people of Muhammad's tribe remembered these events. They were Allah's signs, preparing for belief in Muhammad's prophethood among his own people. Muhammad's father, Abdullah, died before Muhammad ﷺ was born. His mother, Aminah, sent him to live with desert Arabs, as did many noble families. Outside the city in the clean desert air, the children learned courage and independence. The tribes taught them to speak pure Arabic language. Shortly after Muhammad ﷺ returned to his mother, she died. Muhammad ﷺ was an orphan at the age of six.

MUHAMMAD'S YOUTH

His grandfather, Abd Al-Muttalib, loved the boy very much, and took him into his home. Young Muhammad ﷺ went with him everywhere. Abd Al-Muttalib's sons respected his wisdom and age. To honor him, they used to put his chair in the shade of the Kaabah. They sat at his feet and listened to him speak. Once Muhammad ﷺ climbed on his grandfather's place of honor. His uncles scolded him to come down. But Abd Al-Muttalib stopped them, saying, "Leave him! By God, some day he will be a great man."

After his grandfather died, Muhammad ﷺ lived with his uncle, Abu Talib. He was not a rich man, and his family was large. Muhammad ﷺ helped earn his living as a shepherd. He longed to travel with his uncle's caravans to Syria. Abu Talib feared that the desert journey was too hard, but Muhammad ﷺ insisted.

On his first journey, he had many new experiences. When he grew older, he traveled and managed the caravan of a rich Makkan widow named Khadijah.

The caravans passed through ancient cities and ruins. Muhammad ﷺ saw fertile gardens unlike the dry valleys and mountains of home. He heard about struggles between the great empires of Persia and Byzantium to the North and East of Arabia. He learned that Persians worshipped fire and that Byzantium was a Christian empire.

A YOUNG MAN

Muhammad ﷺ grew up loved and respected by the Makkans. He was kind and generous. His honesty earned him the nickname "Al-Sadiq Al-Amin" (the Truthful and Trustworthy). He was a thoughtful person who sought truth. People often asked him for advice. He was well known for his beautiful speech, for generosity and kindness.

Once, his tribe was rebuilding the Kaabah. When it was time to move the sacred black cornerstone, several families competed for the honor. To prevent fighting, they agreed to let Muhammad ﷺ decide among them. He put the stone into a large cloth and told them to raise it all together. He put it in place with his own hands. Everyone was satisfied and peace continued.

A rich widow named Khadijah, respected Muhammad ﷺ. She knew about his good reputation. She was pleased with his work in her trading caravans, which always earned more than expected. Khadijah sent her servant to ask Muhammad ﷺ to marry her. It was a surprising offer. She was rich and he was a poor orphan. She was 40 years old and he was a young man of 25. However, they married and made a happy home with many children.

Understanding Section 2:

1. What was the name of Muhammad's tribe and where was he born?

2. Describe Muhammad's family situation as a child.

3. As a young man, what was his position in his tribe?

4. Who was Khadijah?

Prophet Muhammad ﷺ first received the message of his prophethood in a cave called Hira' near Makkah, where he used to spend time in fasting, prayer and meditation. Through the Angel Jibril, he experienced revelation of the first five verses of Surat Al-'Alaq.

31

Prophethood

During their long life together, Khadijah was friend and support for Muhammad ﷺ. She encouraged his search for truth and belief in Allah. Each year, he spent a month in a mountain cave called Hira'. Far from the town's noise, he thought deeply about the world and man's place in it. He hated the idols his tribe worshipped. He did not share their love of riches. He was saddened by their fighting and the way they treated women and slaves. He longed for a pure, peaceful way of life and worship.

One night, after staying in the cave for many days, Muhammad ﷺ had a terrifying experience. The angel Jibril came to him. Jibril pressed the breath out of him, telling him, "Read!" He said that he was not able to read. The angel repeated and pressed him harder, until he felt he would die. After the third time, the angel said these words, and Muhammad ﷺ understood that he should recite them:

اقْرَأْ بِاسْمِ رَبِّكَ الَّذِى خَلَقَ

خَلَقَ الْإِنسَٰنَ مِنْ عَلَقٍ

اقْرَأْ وَرَبُّكَ الْأَكْرَمُ

الَّذِى عَلَّمَ بِالْقَلَمِ

عَلَّمَ الْإِنسَٰنَ مَا لَمْ يَعْلَمْ

Read: In the name of thy Lord who created,
Created man from a clot.
Read: And thy Lord is most Generous.
Who taught by the pen,
Taught man what he knew not. (Holy Qur'an, 96:1-5)

He left the cave and came home to his wife in a daze. He was shivering and she wrapped him in a cloak. When he was calm, he told her what had happened. He feared that he had lost his mind. Khadijah assured him he was pure and sincere. The Angel must have been from Allah. Khadijah was the first person to believe in Muhammad's prophethood. To help her husband, Khadijah went to her cousin Waraqa to ask his advice about the visit of Jibril. Waraqa was one of the Hunafa', or keepers of belief in one God, and he knew ancient writings that told about the prophets. He told Muhammad ﷺ that his vision had been true. Muhammad ﷺ was chosen by Allah for a great mission. He also told Muhammad ﷺ that his people would make it hard for him. Waraqa, already an old man, promised to help as long as he lived.

For a while, Muhammad ﷺ received no further **revelations** (messages from Allah). Then Jibril came to him in his sleep, saying:

Oh you who lie wrapped in your cloak!
Arise and warn!
Glorify your Lord! (Holy Qur'an, 74:1-3)

Muhammad ﷺ knew that he must tell the people of his family and his tribe about the message.

Muhammad ﷺ was 40 years old when he became a prophet. He felt peaceful that he had found the answer he was seeking. He also felt a heavy responsibility. How would his people act when they heard the message? Would he be able to remain strong?

WHAT ISLAM TAUGHT

Over the next 23 years, Muhammad ﷺ would receive **revelations** from Allah and teach them to the people. The early messages taught that there is One God, named in Arabic **Allah**. The revelation taught that religion means obeying the will of Allah, called **Islam**. A person who submits to God's will is called a **Muslim**. Among the earliest revelations, Muslims learned that Allah would bring everyone to life again and judge their actions after they had died. They would be rewarded with the gardens of **Jannah**, or Heaven, for faith and good behavior. They were also warned of Allah's power to punish them in **Jahannam**, or Hell.

During the next years in Makkah, the Muslims learned how to worship. They learned how to pray and established five regular prayers. They learned that Muhammad ﷺ was the last of many prophets sent by Allah. They heard that Abraham, Jesus, Moses and many others had been prophets. They all taught people to believe in and worship One God, to be kind to parents, the poor, and all of Allah's creatures. Because they had submitted themselves to Allah, the prophets earned the name **Muslim**.

THE MESSAGE SPREADS

The first to accept Muhammad ﷺ as a prophet were his wife Khadijah, his household and a few friends and relatives. The first adult man to become Muslim was Abu Bakr Al- Saddiq, a wealthy and important man of Quraysh. Muhammad ﷺ invited members of his **clan** (family group) to help. They all refused except his young cousin Ali, son of Abu Talib. He called his tribe together at a place outside Makkah, asking if they would believe him if he warned of danger coming from behind the mountain. They replied that he was always truthful. He warned them of Allah's punishment, saying that the danger was just as real as an enemy threatening to attack. Most of them scorned him and refused to believe. When he told the rich Makkan nobles that all men are equal in Allah's eyes, they laughed at him.

Some members of Muhammad's tribe accepted him as prophet and believed in the message. Many of the earliest Muslims were slaves or poor people. Gradually the Muslims increased in number. The Makkan chiefs began to feel threatened. Their power and wealth depended on the pilgrimage. They feared losing these things if they accepted Islam. They thought that their idols brought them luck or misfortune. They were afraid to give up the idols. They felt safer with the old ways of their fathers. Deep inside, many of them felt attracted to Islam and the beautiful Arabic of the message.

PERSECUTION

The Makkan leaders decided to stop the growth of Islam. First they persecuted individual Muslims. They tried everything from insults to torture. Owners punished their Muslim slaves, and a few died. Even these acts failed to make Muslims give up their belief, and their numbers continued to grow. Sons were locked up by their parents for believing in Islam. Wives and husbands disagreed and separated over the truth of the message. Quraysh accused Muhammad ﷺ of breaking up families by teaching Islam. They thought that family loyalty was even more important than truth.

During this time of persecution, Abu Talib protected Muhammad ﷺ from other members of the tribe. As long as Abu Talib lived, they could not risk harming him. The chiefs tried to persuade Abu Talib to stop protecting him. He refused. The chiefs begged Abu Talib to persuade Muhammad ﷺ to stop preaching. They offered him money to stop. They offered to make him king if he wanted power. He refused, saying, "If they gave me the sun in my right hand, and the moon in my left to give up this message, I will not do it unless Allah causes me to die."

During this time, Muhammad ﷺ allowed some of the Muslims to escape from persecution. In small groups, they migrated to a kingdom in Africa, across the Red Sea (now in Ethiopia). The king, named the Negus, was Christian. The Muslims recited the chapter about Jesus' mother, Maryam, from the Qur'an. The Negus wept and promised to protect the Muslims from harm. They stayed in his kingdom for several years.

All of Quraysh's plans had failed, and more members of their tribe were still joining the Muslims. Now the Makkans decided to make the Muslims suffer together. A written order was hung in the Kaabah. The Muslims were sent outside the town. No one was allowed to sell or buy anything from them. They might have starved if some Makkans had not sent them food secretly. After three years, some Makkans convinced their tribe to end this cruelty. Shortly afterward, Muhammad's wife, Khadijah, and uncle Abu Talib died. It was called the Year of Sadness.

THE MURDER PLOT AND MUHAMMAD'S MIGRATION

During each pilgrimage season, Muhammad ﷺ invited visiting tribes to accept the message. Even Quraysh could not prevent this. Some people from the city of Yathrib (see map, p. 14) accepted Islam. The number of followers in Yathrib grew while the Makkans made Muslims' lives more difficult.

After the Year of Sadness, Muhammad ﷺ was shown a place in a dream. It was a land with water and date palms. He knew that this would be the place where the Muslims could go to live, or **emigrate**. During the next pilgrimage, a group of 73 Muslims came to Makkah. They met with Muhammad ﷺ at a place called Aqabah. One year earlier, he had met in the same place with a much smaller group of 12. They promised to follow Islam faithfully. This time, they promised to let the Muslims of Makkah live in their city, and to protect Muhammad ﷺ in peace and in war.

Muhammad ﷺ began sending small groups of Muslims to live in Yathrib. The Makkans feared that Muhammad ﷺ would escape from them, too. If he became a leader in that city, he might threaten their trade or gain power over other tribes. They plotted to bring a warrior from each clan, or family in Quraysh to murder Muhammad ﷺ as one man. That way, Muhammad's own clan could neither resist nor take revenge for his death. Warned of the plot, he escaped secretly to Yathrib with his friend Abu Bakr. He had taught the message of Islam in Makkah for 13 years.

Understanding Section 3:

1. Why did Muhammad ﷺ visit the cave at Hira' each year?

2. What happened to Muhammad in the cave that frightened him?

3. What is a prophet? What other prophets do Muslims also believe in?

4. Did Muhammad's family and tribe accept him as a prophet?

5. What did the leaders of Makkah do when the Muslims began to increase in number?

6. Who offered to help the Muslims? Where did Muhammad ﷺ send the Muslims?

Ten Years in Medinah

This journey from Makkah to Yathrib in 622 is called the **Hijra**, or migration. It marks the beginning of the Muslim calendar, just as the Christian calendar begins with the birth of Jesus. Muhammad's work continued for 10 more years. During those few years, the face of Arabia changed completely.

BUILDING THE COMMUNITY

From the time of the Hijra, the Muslims were able to live as a true community. They still faced many challenges from the Makkans and others, but now they had a place where they could practice Islam without persecution. The name of Yathrib was changed to **Medinat Al-Nabi**, which means City of the Prophet. Muhammad ﷺ became the leader of all the tribes in the city. He drew up a treaty with the two Muslim tribes, called Aws and Khazraj. It also included the Jewish tribes who lived in the city.

The Muslims from Makkah were called **Muhajirun**, or Migrants. Muhammad ﷺ joined each of them with a Muslim of Medina, called **Ansar**, or Helpers. The Muhajirun had left all their property in Makkah. They needed help starting new lives in Medinah. Muhammad ﷺ also wanted the Muslims to learn to live as brothers, even though they belonged to different tribes. It was a new idea for the Arab tribes. Islam taught them that the ties of a common religion are stronger than the ties of blood relationship.

When the Muslim community migrated to Yathrib, the city was renamed Madinat An-Nabi, "City of the Prophet." The Prophet's camel led to the place where the masjid and houses for his family would be built. The pillars and roof beams were trunks of palm trees. The walls were made of earth, and the roof of palm thatch.

A simple **masjid** (place of prayer), was built from palm trunks and mud bricks. The Prophet's house was attached to it. Muslims established the call to prayer, or athan, heard five times a day in Muslim lands all over the world.

A NEW WAY OF LIFE

The message which Muhammad ﷺ received little- by- little over 23 years is called the **Qur'an**. Muslims honor the **Qur'an** as a mercy from Allah. The **Qur'an** teaches that a sign of Allah's love is showing people, or **revealing** how to live a pure and good life. To a Muslim, **Islam** means obeying Allah by following the path, or way of life that He intended. Many **Qur'an** verses revealed while the Prophet lived in Medinah contain guidance about building the Islamic community. These include many longer chapters, or **surahs**.

The verses revealed in Medinah explain many principles, or general ideas about how a community should work. They explain many details about the rights and duties of each citizen. Families are the building blocks of a community. **Qur'an** verses describe the duties and rights of each member. Everyone must be provided for and protected. Conditions for marriage and inheriting property after death are clearly stated. Muslims are commanded to share their wealth with the poor. Some verses tell how to be fair in trade, and how to prevent crimes like stealing and murder. Other verses order Muslims to keep agreements and good relations with other communities.

MANY TRADITIONS CHANGE

These rules became the new community's laws. Some rules agreed with people's traditions and customs before Islam. However, many of the new rules required big changes. Because of their strong belief in Allah, they got rid of very old traditions just as they got rid of the Muslims idols. Part of being Muslim is promising to obey what Allah and His Prophet tell us to do.

One big change was in the way women were treated. Before Islam, women had a low position in Arab society. If a baby girl was born, the husband became sad and ashamed. Sometimes the baby was buried alive before anyone found out. They only wanted sons. A wife was her husband's property, and she did not have rights.

Muhammad ﷺ ended the killing of baby girls. He taught men to respect women and give them rights. Women can speak out and take part in the community. Money that they inherit or earn is theirs to keep. Women can own, buy and sell land or goods. Most important, Islam taught that men and women are equal before Allah.

Another big change took place in Medinah. The Arabs had loved to drink wine and gamble. Some even sold themselves into slavery by losing a game! Muslims were told that these things are dangerous for a person and for the community. When the order came to give them up, the Muslims obeyed. They were taught to live a pure, healthy life.

BATTLES AND TREATIES

Unhappy that Muhammad ﷺ had escaped their murder plot, the Makkan leaders now watched the Muslims in Medinah carefully. When they heard of Muhammad's treaty with tribes in and near Medinah, Quraysh prepared themselves to fight. They saw the treaty as a threat to their power in Arabia. The Makkans looked for a way to weaken the treaty. Quraysh's own weak spot was that their caravans must pass by Medinah. If Muslims were friendly with tribes through whose territory the caravans passed, their trade was threatened. How much worse for Quraysh if some of these tribes accepted Islam! Quraysh would try to destroy the Muslims in war.

On their side, the Muhajirun had not wanted to leave Makkah. It was their home, and Quraysh were their families. They had suffered for 13 years in Makkah without raising weapons in defense. Many of them had lost their businesses, wealth and houses. After the Muslims migrated, Quraysh took over their property.

The Muslims knew that Quraysh would not leave them alone. New Muslims were coming to Medinah from Quraysh and other tribes. The Muslims wanted Quraysh to make a treaty. It would allow them to teach Islam to other tribes. Without a treaty, the tribes would be afraid of powerful Quraysh. A treaty would make Quraysh admit that Muhammad ﷺ and the Muslims were an independent power. That was a bitter pill for the chiefs of Quraysh to swallow. They wanted to show other Arab tribes that the Muslims were weak refugees thrown out by their own tribe.

To show the Muslims' strength, small groups were sent out from Medina. Without fighting, they threatened Makkan caravans and made treaties with nearby tribes. Later a Makkan was killed. Quraysh accused the Muslims of fighting during the forbidden months of caravan travel. Then a Qur'an verse came which gave the Muslims permission to fight. It declared that war and killing are evil, but keeping people from faith in Allah is worse. The Makkans had certainly tried to do that. Muslims won the first battle, called Badr. One year later, at Uhud, they almost lost the battle, and Muhammad ﷺ was wounded. After two years, Quraysh and their allies brought a large army to attack Medina. The Muslims defended their city with a big ditch. Unable to cross the ditch, the Makkans camped and waited. Finally, a storm broke up their camp and the Makkan armies went home in defeat.

During the years of battle, tribes and individuals accepted Islam. Some made peace treaties with the Muslims. Muslim teachers were sent to explain Islam and teach the Qur'an to new Muslims. Other tribes remained allies of Quraysh, and some tried to harm the Muslims.

After many years in Medinah, the Muhajirun missed their home in Makkah. Muhammad ﷺ longed to make pilgrimage to the Kaabah. Unarmed, Muhammad ﷺ and the Muslims set out to visit Makkah. That year, the Quryash did not let them enter, but a treaty was finally made. The treaty allowed any tribe to join the Muslims without fear of attack. Quraysh now admitted that the Muslims were very strong. Muhammad ﷺ had reached his goal.

VICTORY AND THE END OF MUHAMMAD'S LIFE

Less than two years later, Quraysh broke the treaty, and an army of 10,000 Muslims marched to Makkah. When they saw the large number of tribes in full battle dress, the embarrassed Makkan leaders finally gave up the struggle against Islam. Muhammad ﷺ offered protection to anyone who stayed in their houses. The Muslims entered the city without fighting. Instead of punishing Quraysh for years of bloodshed, Muhammad ﷺ forgave his tribe. He cleaned all the idols out of the Kaabah and purified it. Since that day, the Kaabah has been a place of Islamic worship.

After the victory at Makkah, which Quraysh hardly resisted, Muhammad ﷺ and his companions cleared out the idols from the Ka'abah. Bilal stood atop the Ka'abah and made adhan. Since that day, the Ka'abah has been a place for worshipping only Allah. Muhammad ﷺ forgave the people of his tribe.

In the following years, most of the tribes in Arabia joined Islam. There were more battles, and the new Muslims of Quraysh joined the Muslim armies. Muhammad ﷺ sent letters to kings in the great empires, inviting them to Islam. Some accepted, while others replied with presents and letters. Some refused and even replied with insults. A Muslim army of 30,000 was sent to meet the Romans for the first time at a place called Tabuk. Although no fighting took place, it would not be the last meeting with Rome. New treaties were made with tribes along the way. The fame of the Muslims and the message of Islam spread further.

In 632, Muhammad ﷺ made Hajj, or pilgrimage, to the Kaabah for the last time. He gave a farewell speech, warning his people of many difficulties to come. He told them to remain true to their Islamic beliefs. A short time later Muhammad ﷺ died. Muslims were extremely sad. Some even refused to believe that their prophet could die.

Abu Bakr, Muhammad's constant friend, told the people, "Whoever worshipped Muhammad ﷺ, he is dead. Whoever worships Allah, He is alive and does not die." He reminded them of a verse from the Qur'an:

وَمَا مُحَمَّدٌ
إِلَّا رَسُولٌ قَدْ خَلَتْ مِن قَبْلِهِ الرُّسُلُ أَفَإِين مَّاتَ أَوْ قُتِلَ
انقَلَبْتُمْ عَلَىٰ أَعْقَابِكُمْ وَمَن يَنقَلِبْ عَلَىٰ عَقِبَيْهِ فَلَن يَضُرَّ
اللَّهَ شَيْئًا وَسَيَجْزِي اللَّهُ الشَّاكِرِينَ

Muhammad is only a messenger,
like those who passed away before him.
If he dies or is killed, will you turn back? (Qur'an, 3:144)

ISLAM AFTER MUHAMMAD—A GREAT RESPONSIBILITY

Muhammad ﷺ had been prophet, leader, judge and teacher. Although his community had become very wealthy, he lived simply and left no possessions when he died. He left behind a government of just laws. He left a community with rules for relations between citizens. He left a model for a way of life.

He had taught that this is the way to worship and please Allah, to gain peace in this life and success in the life to come. Muslims would continue Muhammad's work. They would meet new problems, and must decide what their prophet would have done. In his last speech, Muhammad ﷺ had told the Muslims, "Those who are here should give the message to those who are absent." They believed it was their duty to carry the message to all people. It was a great challenge.

Understanding Section 4:

1. What event marks the beginning of the Muslim calendar? What is the date according to the Christian calendar?

2. In what way did the Muslims' situation improve at Medinah?

3. Name the two groups in Medinah who formed a brotherhood. What do their names mean?

4. Name the message which Muslims honor as Allah's word. How long did it take to complete the Qur'an?

5. List two laws of the Muslim community that came from the Qur'an.

6. Name two big changes which Islam brought to the Muslims' way of life.

7. Tell what each side, Quraysh and the Muslims, wanted to do that brought them to the point of war. Why?

8. What victory did the Muslims win without fighting? What did Muhammad ﷺ do after he entered the city?

9. How far did Islam spread by the end of Muhammad's life?

ISLAM AND MUSLIM CIVILIZATION

CHAPTER TWO

"Muslim Civilization"

Written by Susan Douglass
Illustrated by Abd Al-Muttalib Fahemy and Susan Douglass

Muslim Civilization

وَلْتَكُن مِّنكُمْ أُمَّةٌ يَدْعُونَ إِلَى ٱلْخَيْرِ وَيَأْمُرُونَ بِٱلْمَعْرُوفِ وَيَنْهَوْنَ عَنِ ٱلْمُنكَرِ وَأُوْلَٰٓئِكَ هُمُ ٱلْمُفْلِحُونَ

And let there be from you a nation,
Inviting to all that is good,
Enjoining what is right and forbidding what is wrong;
Such are they who are successful. (Qur'an 3:104)

Muhammad ﷺ was a humble man who never learned to read and write. Yet scholars spend their lives studying the message that Allah revealed to him. He recited verses whose beauty and wisdom is a measure for poets. He led Arabia during his lifetime. He became a model for millions of people all over the world. In this chapter, we will explore history from about 1000 years after Muhammad's death in 632. We will study the civilization that Muslims built. We will see how they tried to meet Islam's high standards.

Jihad means "to make an effort." Anything a Muslim does requires an effort to overcome difficulties. The main difficulty in spreading Islam was that some rulers did not want their people to hear about Islam. These rulers wanted to decide the faith of their subjects. Those who disagreed suffered persecution. Muslim soldiers fought to open these lands to Islam by making treaties or defeating these rulers.

48

Part III:

Student Text
Chapter Two

Expansion and the Spread of Islam

After Muhammad's death, Islam spread beyond the borders of Arabia. In less than 100 years, the small community had spread to Asia, Africa and Europe. Military victories carried Islam rapidly across these continents. Two empires fell in its path. Trade and science carried Islam even further. In this section, we will explore how the Muslim lands expanded.

FIGHTING AGAINST PERSECUTION

The Arabic word **jihad** means to make an effort. Islam teaches that the most difficult jihad is trying to be a good person. Jihad also means fighting to defend Islam. The Qur'an permits fighting against **persecution**. When people are **persecuted**, they are not allowed to practice or tell others about their faith. Freedom of religion or speech was not guaranteed then. People had to follow the religion of their king or risk trouble. Quraysh had persecuted Muhammad and his followers. In the Roman and Persian Empires, Jews and Christians often suffered prison or death if their beliefs were different from the emperor's.

To invite people to Islam, it was necessary to persuade or defeat their leaders. Before any fighting, leaders were invited to learn about Islam. They were asked to let Muslims spread the message freely. They were asked to let people practice their chosen faith. If they refused, Muslim armies fought to open these lands to the Islamic message.

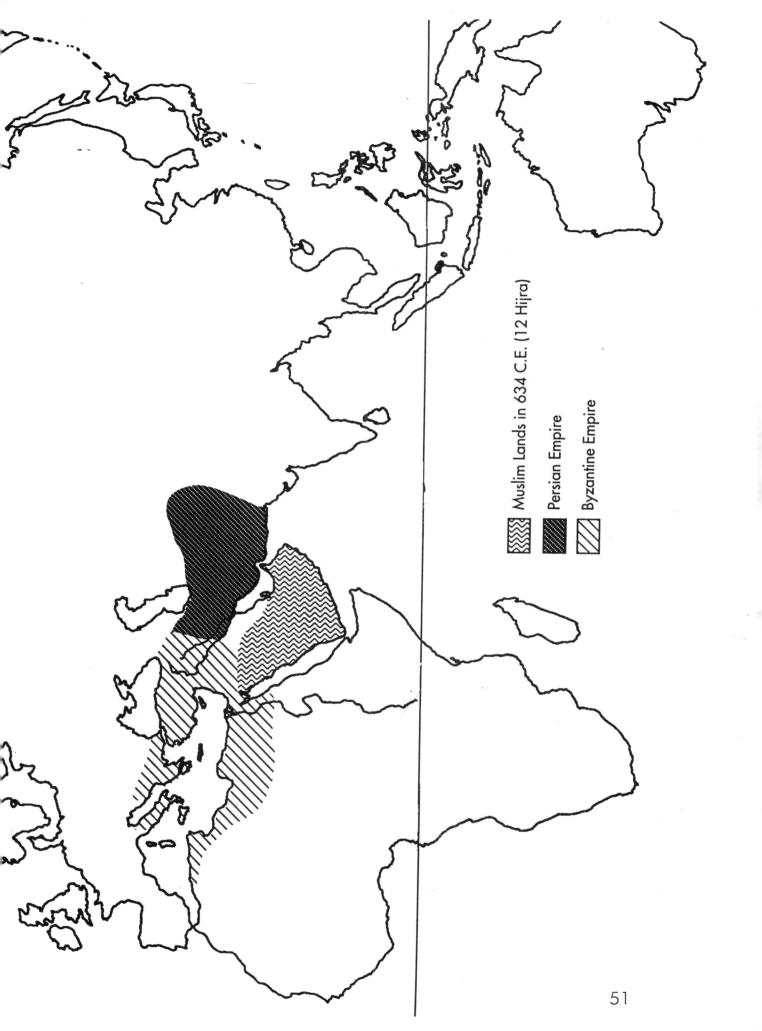

Muslim Lands in 634 C.E. (12 Hijra)

Persian Empire

Byzantine Empire

51

Islam forbids forcing others to become Muslim during **jihad**. A person should accept Islam because he or she is convinced that it is true. A person is Muslim in Allah's eyes only if he or she is sincere. The Qur'an says:

لَآ إِكْرَاهَ فِى ٱلدِّينِ قَد تَّبَيَّنَ ٱلرُّشْدُ مِنَ ٱلْغَىِّ

Let there be no compulsion in religion,
Truth stands out clearly from error. (Qur'an 2:256)

CONDITIONS FOR WAR IN ISLAM

Islam permitted fighting only under strict conditions. The Qur'an forbids starting a war to capture land or goods. Armies may fight against soldiers, but not attack towns, villages, or unarmed folk. Children, women, and old people must be protected. Armies must not steal supplies or destroy crops and animals. Prisoners must be treated well. Captured goods must be divided fairly, including a part for charity.

Throughout most of history, there were no such controls on fighting. War was terrible for people in cities and countryside. Opposing armies trampled back and forth across the land. It did not matter much who won. Victory for either side meant destruction first, then heavy taxes.

MUSLIM ARMIES DEFEAT EMPIRES

The Persian and Byzantine Empires were weak from constant fighting. Jews, Christians and other groups suffered persecution. Expensive armies used up tax money. War interrupted trade, destroying cities and farm land. Taxes meant great hardship for citizens. Many people were unhappy with their rulers.

Some Arab tribes on the edges of the two empires joined the Muslims. Others wanted independence. Some Arabs fought against the Muslim armies at first. Both empires watched events in Arabia. They never expected desert tribes to defeat great powers like themselves.

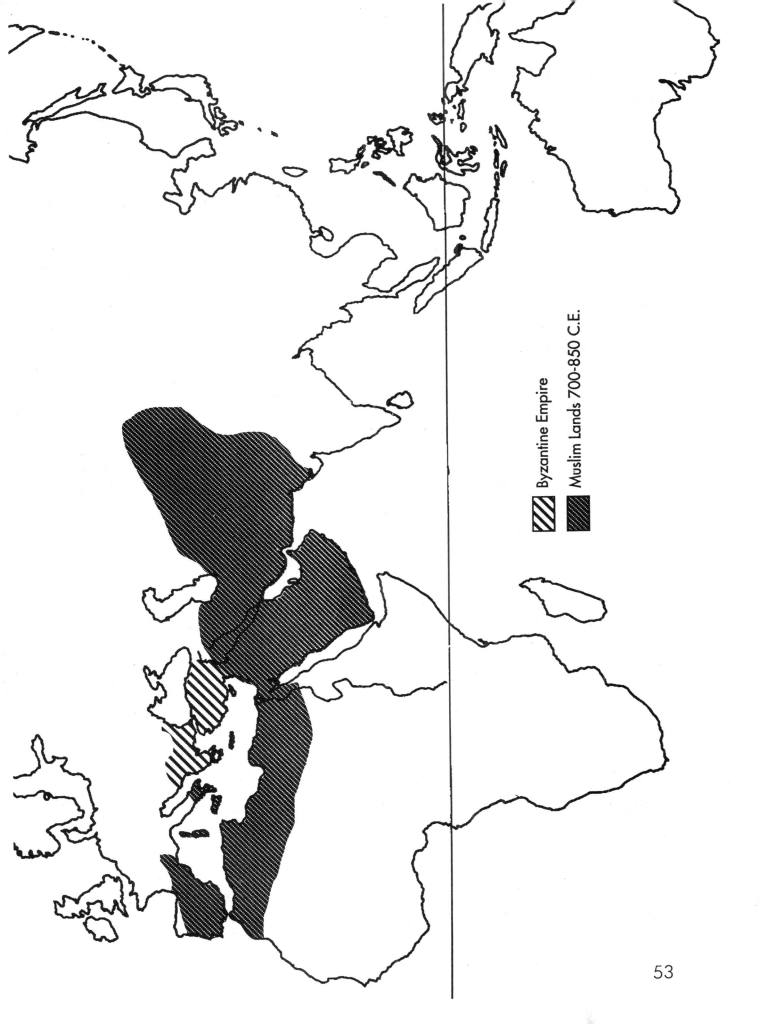

Byzantine Empire

Muslim Lands 700-850 C.E.

The Muslim state expanded in two directions at once. In the Northwest, Muslim armies took Palestine and Syria from the Byzantines in 637. Khalifah Umar Ibn Al-Khattab accepted the keys to Jerusalem. In the Northeast, Muslims defeated the Persian army near the Tigris-Euphrates River. (See map, p. 43.)

Muslim armies kept moving east and west. The Persians lost the heart of their empire in heavy fighting. Persians fought with heavy equipment and elephants. The Muslims' faith gave them strong fighting spirit. Their light armor, quick horses and camels were effective in desert battles. By 651, the Persian empire was finished. The last emperor was killed by his own general.

In the West, the Muslim army took Egypt. They camped on the Nile River where the delta begins, founding the city of Cairo. With the help of Syrian and Egyptian seamen, they built a navy. Together they defeated the Byzantine navy. Cyprus, Sicily, and other islands in the Mediterranean added to Muslim lands.

By 711, the Muslims had moved across North Africa to the Atlantic Ocean. Many nomadic **Berber** tribesmen of the Sahara desert accepted Islam. They joined the troops who carried Islam to Spain. By 732 they reached southern France and Switzerland. Muslims ruled in Spain (**Al-Andalus**) for 700 years, until 1492.

Parts of northern India came under Muslim rule. By 750, Muslims stood at the borders of China on important Asian trade routes.

In a little more than 100 years, lands from the Atlantic Ocean to China were open to Islam. Two empires had fallen. Many people accepted Islam and began to change their way of life. Other religious groups practiced their faiths in safety. Many of these accepted Islam much later. (See map, p. 47)

Islam continued to spread steadily. The strength and size of the Muslim state attracted many to Islam. Scholars' books spread Islamic ideas far beyond their borders. Islam spread along trade routes by land and sea.

Traders spread their religion and way of life by example. They carried Islam deep into Asia on the Silk Road. They brought it to the coasts of India and Africa, to Southeast Asia and the Spice Islands. Caravans brought Islam

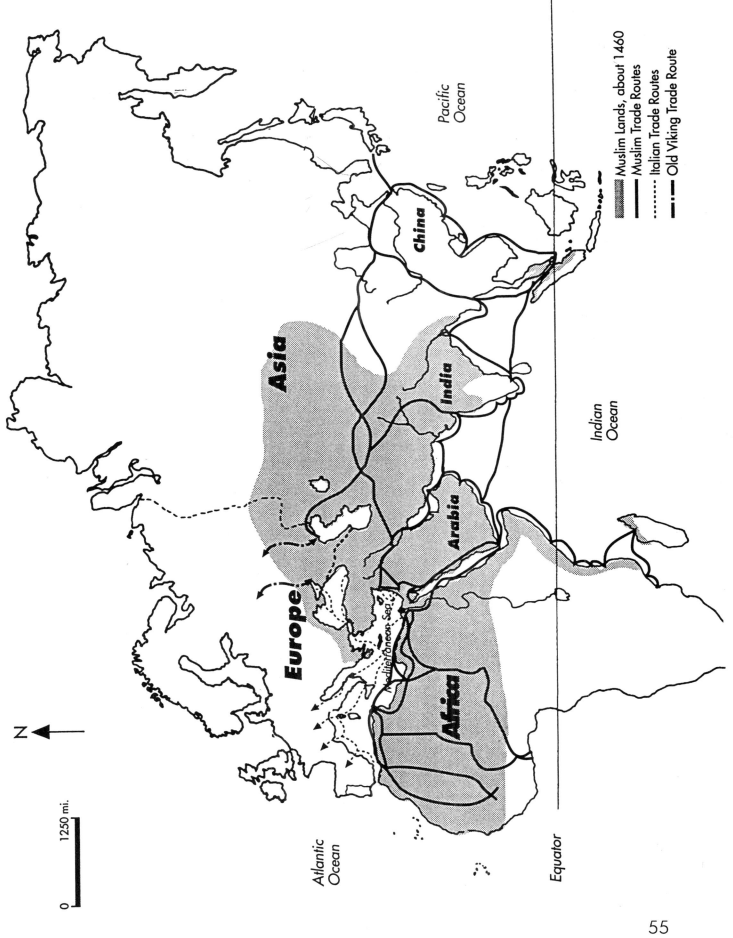

N

1250 mi.

0

Atlantic
Ocean

Europe

Mediterranean Sea

Africa

Arabia

India

Asia

China

Pacific
Ocean

Indian
Ocean

Equator

Muslim Lands, about 1460

Muslim Trade Routes

Italian Trade Routes

Old Viking Trade Route

across the Sahara Desert to West Africa. Wherever Muslim traders went, they built **masajid** (mosques). Scholars and judges followed. By trading with Muslim merchants, people learned Islamic laws and Arabic language. Many were attracted to the simple faith. (See map, p. 47)

Islam is still growing. Muslims travel to Europe and North America to study or find work. As they did long ago, Muslims bring along their way of life and worship. Some citizens of Western countries have accepted Islam. Fourteen centuries after Muhammad ﷺ, people are still learning about the message of Islam.

Understanding Section 1:

1. Give an example of religious persecution long ago.

2. Why did Islam permit fighting?

3. Why does Islam place strict conditions on Muslim armies?

4. List several reasons why the Persian and Byzantine Empires were weak.

5. From each of the following pairs, choose the land that came under Islamic rule first:

   a. Palestine —— Persia

   b. India —— Egypt

   c. Southern France —— North Africa

6. How long did the Muslims rule Spain? For extra credit, what other historic event happened in 1492?

7. Name three ways by which Islam spread to other lands.

Governing the Lands by Islam

What problems did the new Muslim rulers face? First, the Muslim lands expanded very fast. The state stretched from the Atlantic Ocean to China, a journey of several months. Communication was no faster than a swift horse. Second, the people of these lands had diverse (or differing) cultures and traditions. Some were nomads like the Arab tribes, or farmed in villages. Others lived by trading in cities. They had different languages and religions. Third, the new lands also had **diverse** geography. Arabia, Saharan Africa and parts of Asia were deserts. Some places had enough rain for farming. Other lands, like Egypt and Iraq, needed irrigation. It would take time to join many lands and peoples under one government.

THE TASK OF GOVERNING

Think of the early Muslim state as a tug-of-war. On one side, the Arabs brought a new system. Ideas of equality and justice must become practical ways of ruling. The state needed **authority** (strong and respected leadership). Advisors to the ruler should represent many groups. Local governments must collect taxes and keep order. The state needed just laws, with courts to enforce them. In Islam, laws must apply equally to rich and poor. An army must protect the state without becoming too powerful. Communication and education must connect many lands and peoples into one body.

On the other side of the tug-of-war were people and traditions. People were used to kings in the old empires. The wealthy enjoyed a fashionable life in fine palaces. Most people expected the new rulers to act like their old ones.

Wealth acted like a great weight pulling against the Muslims. The Qur'an and Muhammad ﷺ warned that riches can divide people. Wealth can bring hatred and envy. Some Muslims began to compete for the power that wealth can bring.

ARABS GOVERN THE NEW LANDS

After the Persians' and the Byzantines' defeat, their citizens were hopeful. Muslim leaders offered the cities protection. Land and common people were safe. Jews, Christians and other groups practiced their religions. Most citizens paid less in taxes. If these people had fought against Islamic rule, the Muslim lands could not have expanded so fast. The Arab armies were not large enough to control the new lands and expand at the same time.

Arabs migrated to the new lands. Army camps turned into towns as soldiers built homes and **masajid** (mosques). Neighboring people joined them. Makkan traders settled in fertile Syria, joining their long-time trade partners.

The Arabs' knowledge of Islam made them best suited to govern the new state. In time, other groups would enter Islam and share power with the Arabs. From the start, Arab rulers needed help from local people. Their governments needed many officials, and most government records were written in Greek or Persian. Arabs kept many officials who had served the Persian and Byzantine empires. It took many years to change these old systems and find new Islamic ways.

THE RIGHTLY GUIDED KHALIFAHS

After the death of their Prophet, the Muslims had to choose a new leader. They called the leader **Khalifah**. That means successor to Muhammad ﷺ. However, the Khalifah would not receive revelation like a prophet. His job was to lead Muslims by following the Qur'an and Muhammad's example.

The first four rulers of the Muslim state are known as the **Rightly Guided Khalifahs**. In 632, the community chose Abu Bakr as Khalifah. When Abu Bakr died two years later, Umar Ibn Al-Khattab ruled for 10 years. Then Uthman Ibn 'Affan served for 12 years. Ali Ibn Abi Talib was Khalifah for 5 years. These leaders governed the Muslims for almost 30 years, until 661.

The Rightly Guided Khalifahs lived simply. They gave wealth rather than taking from the treasury for themselves. With wisdom, courage, and knowledge of Islam, they sought solutions to new problems. They felt responsible for the good of all the people. They made careful decisions for the future. Historians still admire these leaders and learn from their wisdom. From 717 to 720, a Khalifah named Umar Ibn Abd Al- Aziz also ruled very justly. He is called the fifth Rightly Guided Khalifah.

They worked hard to govern well. Their capital was at Madinah, far away from the lands they controlled. They began projects to connect the Muslim lands. They tried to appoint wise and honest officials to serve the people. They listened to advisors and heard advice from rich and poor alike.

In spite of the Khalifahs' care, some governors gathered too much power. People complained of injustices. Although the Khalifahs tried, these governors were difficult to control. Wealthy and powerful people supported these governors, and they became too strong for the Khalifah to control.

The period of the Rightly Guided Khalifahs ended with a time of dispute, called **fitnah** in the Muslim community. There was a conflict over who should be Khalifah after Uthman Ibn 'Affan. Some officials appointed by Uthman as governors were not behaving as Muslim leaders should. Competition over land and wealth caused jealousy between groups in the growing state. A group of soldiers from the provinces murdered Uthman in his house. When Ali Ibn Abi Talib was chosen Khalifah, some people did not accept him. Trouble came from Syria. Its governor was Mu'awiya, a man from Uthman's family. He had many wealthy supporters. A relative of Uthman, Mu'awiya wanted his murder punished. Mu'awiyah declared himself rival Khalifah. Civil war threatened. Khalifah Ali moved the capital city to Iraq.

After several years, the bitter dispute continued to disturb the state. Respected companions of Muhammad ﷺ were horrified by the situation. They did not want to take sides. They tried to find the best way to keep the Islamic state united.

After five years as Khalifah, Ali Ibn Abi Talib was murdered. Mu'awiyah's position as Khalifah became stronger. Later, when Mu'awiyah's son Yazid ruled the Muslim state, Ali's followers in Iraq rebelled. At Karbala, in the Iraqi desert, the Prophet's grandson Husayn was killed. The event shocked the Muslim community deeply. Even now, Muslims feel great sadness over this event. The **fitnah** events would disturb the Islamic community for many generations to come.

THE UMAYYAD RULERS

Mu'awiyah moved the official capital to Damascus, where his supporters were. Mu'awiyah also changed the way of choosing the Khalifah. He failed to let the community choose among its best leaders. Instead, he named his son, Yazid. They founded a **dynasty**, or rule by a family through many generations. The Umayyad dynasty ruled for about 130 years, until 750.

The Umayyads were more like the kings their subjects were used to. They lived in palaces, enjoying the arts and luxuries of the imperial city. Military troops in Syria supported the Umayyad rulers. They were harsh with people who disagreed with them. Unity was enforced with might. The Umayyad rulers became more distant from the people they ruled.

Umayyad rule benefited the Muslim lands. They built roads, canals and harbors. They had a postal system like the pony express. They changed official record-keeping to Arabic language. Arts and sciences began to develop, along with the system of Islamic law. The state expanded rapidly under Umayyad rule.

THE ABBASSIDS START A NEW DYNASTY

The next ruling family was called the Abbassids. Their supporters were new converts to Islam. They wanted to share power with the ruling Arabs. Many other Muslims also hoped for change. But when Abbassid rulers came to power, they became like emperors. The last member of the Umayyad family fled to **Al-Andalus** after his family was killed. They built a dynasty at the city of **Cordoba**.

The splendid city of **Baghdad** was built as the Abbassid capital in Iraq. It became a great center of administration and trade. The Abbassid court set fashions for luxury and style in art and poetry. Abbassid rulers built mosques, roads, hospitals and places for pilgrims and traders to rest. They spent freely on arts and learning, too. Fine libraries, schools, universities and hospitals were built during their rule.

This is how an artist thinks the Round City, the Abbasid rulers' capital at Baghdad may have looked. The city-within-a-city held the entire government. In the center was the khalifah's palace and masjid. The inner ring of buildings housed his family and high officials. The outer ring held government offices, libraries, housing and markets (The shops were later moved out.). Around the outside were double walls, and four gates leading to important lands of the Muslim state. The Tigris River flows by, and the busy city of Baghdad, with its many canals, spread out around the Round City. It was the only round-shaped city in the world. To draw this picturem the artist had to study descriptions of the place by Muslim writers from long ago and modern historians.

Muhammad ﷺ had led the prayer and worked side by side with his people. The Abbassids ruled from behind high palace walls. Jealous officials and luxury kept them far from ordinary people. Many Muslims were shocked to see people kiss the ground and bow before them. This was the ignorance which Islam had come to destroy. Muslims are supposed to bow down only to Allah. The Muslim lands were rich and powerful, so most people accepted Abbassid rule, but many Muslims felt that some of the Abbassid rulers' ways were against Islamic teaching.

GOVERNMENT BREAKS UP INTO SMALL STATES

Many groups opposed the Abbassid rulers. In time, the government broke up into small states ruled by princes and governors. They looked to the Khalifah as leader of the Muslims, but they considered their own interests before all others. By 945, they were really independent rulers, and the Khalifah had become just a figure. In Egypt and Spain, opposing dynasties ruled. In the lands between, many jealous princes ruled over cities, castles and their countryside. They often fought among each other.

The Islamic state lost its unity. Many of its leaders forgot the example of Prophet Muhammad ﷺ. Invaders took over some of the Muslim lands. One example of these losses was Spain. Christian kings and soldiers took cities and lands of Muslim Spain. Gradually, the Muslims were pushed out of Spain completely by 1492.

Another example was the **Crusades**. Crusaders were European Christian armies sent by the Church in Rome. They wanted to capture Jerusalem and surrounding lands where Jesus had lived. These wars started in about 1100 and ended just before 1300. During the Crusades, important Muslim cities like Aleppo, Damascus, and even Jerusalem fell to the Christians. Crusader armies took advantage of disunity in the Muslim lands. Their knights and nobles set up governments in those places. Many Muslims, Jews and even Eastern Christians lost their lives. Finally, the Crusader States fell and the land returned to Muslim rule.

Even long ago, Muslim doctors practiced medicine in hospitals. They uses medicines from plants grown in the hospital herb garden or brought from distant lands. They performed surgery with instruments they invented. Some of these are still used today. Poor people were treated without paying. Muslim doctors even treated some Christian knights during the Crusades. Muslim medical books were used in many lands.

NOMADIC WARRIORS FROM CENTRAL ASIA

After the Abbassids, tribes of Central Asian nomads played important roles in Islam. They came as warriors and invaders, and later became Muslims. They set up governments and contributed to Muslim culture. These Turkish and Mongol tribes brought huge lands into the fold of Islam.

The first important tribe was the Seljuk Turks. They were brave and skilled soldiers whom the Abbassids used as guards. In time, the Abbassid rulers depended upon these soldiers to keep them in power. Finally, they even chose the Khalifah. In 945, the Seljuks took the city of Baghdad. They set up a dynasty in eastern Muslim lands.

In the 1200s, a great disaster happened in Europe and Asia. Central Asian nomads called the **Mongols** began a great invasion. They were skilled horsemen, loyal tribesmen, and fierce warriors. They formed an efficient military machine that rolled over China, Europe and the eastern Muslim lands. They destroyed Baghdad in 1258. Muslim troops finally stopped the Mongols in a famous battle at Ain Jalut ("Eye of Goliath") in Palestine.

In a short time the Mongols built the largest empire the world had ever seen. The Mongol Empire did not last. In less than 100 years, their state broke up. By the 1300s, most of the Mongols had become Muslims. They set up governments in Persia, India, and Russia. They brought Muslim scholars and judges to their royal courts. Beautiful buildings, books and works of art soon appeared. The Mongols, or Mughals, ruled most of India until the British conquered them in the 1800s.

OTTOMAN TURKS RULE

In 1326, a Muslim group called the Ottomans took over Byzantine Turkey. The group is named after one of its important leaders, Osman (Uthman). In 1453, they took Constantinople and renamed it **Istanbul**. Then they expanded in all directions. Much of Eastern Europe, the Mediterranean lands and Arabia came under Ottoman control.

Ottoman rule did much to restore unity to the Muslim lands. The arts, sciences and building flowered again. Trade and craft goods from Ottoman lands were

The qadi, or judge, was a very important person in Muslim society. Muslim judges were scholars in sharia'h, or Islamic law. They helped govern and keep peace in Muslim lands. They settled disagreements between individuals and families. Men and women brought their cases, such as marriage, crimes, land and goods to be decided by the qadi.

known around the world. Their well-organized army became a model for European armies. The Ottoman state included people of many cultures, religions and languages. Their system of government lasted until the 20th century.

Many smaller states in Asia, Africa and the Spice Islands governed Muslims until modern times. You may study some of these states when you learn about Africa and Southern Asia.

Understanding Section 2:

1. List two problems faced by the rulers of the Muslim lands.

2. Why were Arabs the first rulers of the Muslim state?

3. What were the first four Khalifahs called? Why?

4. How is the ruler chosen in a **dynasty**? How does that differ from the way the first four Khalifahs were chosen?

5. In what ways were the Umayyad and Abbassid Dynasties different from the early Khalifahs?

6. Which two groups of skilled soldiers from Central Asia accepted Islam and ruled over Muslim territories?

7. What was the name for the Mongol rulers in India?

8. What Muslim ruling group renamed Constantinople in 1458, and ruled until the 20th century?

The Spread of Knowledge

Spreading Islam meant teaching about the faith. The Qur'an forbids Muslims from forcing others to accept Islam. They must use reason, and try to be living examples like their prophet. The first step was to preserve and pass on knowledge about Islam. From that beginning, Muslims started a revolution in knowledge and science that changed the world.

PRESERVING KNOWLEDGE

The Qur'an is the most important source of knowledge about Islam. It was revealed over the 23 years of Muhammad's prophethood. Whenever new verses were revealed to Muhammad ﷺ, his companions memorized and wrote them down. Muslims recite Qur'an in their five daily prayers. Each year during the month of Ramadan, the companions recited the Qur'an from beginning to end. Muhammad ﷺ recited it and heard the companions recite it. By the time of Muhammad's death, hundreds of people knew the whole Qur'an by heart.

After his death, the Qur'an was carefully preserved. Muhammad's followers taught others to recite it in the same way they had heard it. The early Khalifahs had the complete Qur'an checked and collected into a book. Zaid Ibn Thabit was in charge of that job. He had learned the Qur'an directly from Prophet Muhammad ﷺ. Another problem came when Islam spread to non-Arab lands. Scholars improved the system of writing Arabic to prevent accidental changes in the Qur'an.

Those who knew how to write among Prophet Muhammad's companions, or sahabah, memorized and wrote down verses of the Qur'an as the Prophet recited them after revelation. Those who could not write memorized them only. The companions did the same with hadith, or sayings and deeds of the Prophet.

All Muslims learn to recite Qur'an in Arabic. People who speak other languages use translations to help them understand the meaning. Even today, the Qur'an is the same all over the world.

The second source of Islamic knowledge is Muhammad's example, the **Sunnah**. Sayings and deeds of Muhammad ﷺ, called **hadith**, were memorized while he was still alive. Later Muslims collected them into books. They recorded all the names of people who passed down the hadith from Muhammad's generation. Two of the most famous collectors were *Muslim* and *Bukhari*. Today, many libraries contain these and other collections.

MUSLIM SCHOLARS KEPT ISLAM STRONG

As the Islamic state became more powerful and worldly, many Muslims were dissatisfied. They did not like the way their rulers lived and governed. These Muslims did not give up Islam's high ideals. They worked to improve government. They sought ways to keep an Islamic spirit in the changing state.

Muslim scholars developed a system based on 'ilm (knowledge). Study of Arabic grammar helped explain the Qur'an. They collected the history of Muhammad's life and community, called the **Sirah**. They checked and collected a record of Muhammad's deeds and sayings, the **Hadith**. They made careful rules for explaining the **Qur'an** and Muhammad's example, the **Sunnah**. They used these rules to discover how Muslims and their leaders should act.

The science of **fiqh** (understanding) developed from this information. **Fiqh** is a practical guide for personal and community behavior. Fiqh contains guidelines for a complete Muslim society.

From this knowledge, Islamic **Shari'ah** developed. Shari'ah is a system of law based on Qur'an and Sunnah. The Shari'ah contains principles of government, economics and justice. It has a system of social law. It guides relations between different countries and religious groups. The Shari'ah shows Muslim leaders how to keep an Islamic system of life as society changes over time.

The work of Muslim scholars set Islamic standards for governments and individuals. Their careful work united the Muslim community in basic agreement.

Muslim astronomers studied the stars from observatories like this one. These carefully placed plat-
forms helped astronomers make accurate measurements of the movement of stars and planets.
These astronomers developed mathematics and instruments that helped people pray towards
Makkah, sail the seas on long journeys, measure the size of the earth and begin to understand our
universe. Without their work, modern people may never have made it to the moon!

People could hold their leaders up to this high standard. Muslim governments could not ignore it.

Some rulers tried harder than others to meet this standard. Many Muslim governments have not applied the Shari'ah closely. Shari'ah law has been strongest in the courts that govern Muslims' everyday life. Today, Muslim scholars still work to meet modern needs using Islamic Shari'ah.

STUDY OF THE QUR'AN LED TO SCIENCE

In the last section, you read how studying the Qur'an led to Islamic **Shari'ah**. Studying the Qur'an also led to exploration of science.

Muslim scholars studied the Qur'an as the key to knowledge. Many verses describe nature, the stars and planets, and changes in the earth. There are clues about medicine, biology and history. Muslim thinkers found new ideas in the Qur'an.

Muhammad ﷺ told Muslims to go even to China for knowledge. The Qur'an invites people to discover how the natural world works. The Qur'an tells that creation obeys Allah's laws. People can understand these laws by using the powers He gave them. In following centuries, Muslim scientists took up this challenge. They brought together knowledge from many cultures. Adding their own work, they passed this knowledge along to others.

SCHOLARS GATHER KNOWLEDGE FROM MANY CULTURES

When Islam spread to Byzantine and Persian lands, Muslims discovered knowledge from other civilizations. The Muslim lands had a rich history of Greek, Persian and Roman culture. As Islam moved toward India and China, Muslims picked up knowledge from those cultures. Libraries were preserved and not burned as they have been by many armies in history.

Scholars of other religions worked with Muslims as teachers and translators. Translating knowledge into Arabic began under the first four Khalifahs. It grew under the Abbassid rulers, and Islamic science flowered. Baghdad was a

Scholars in Muslim lands gathered knowledge from many civilizations. They read and translated ancient and newer books into Arabic. Men and women wrote about those subjects and developed new knowledge, science and literature. Libraries with thousands of books were places where scholars met to share ideas.

center of scholarship. The Khalifah founded the House of Wisdom in 830. It was a library, academy, museum and translation center all in one. Works of ancient Greek philosophers, mathematicians, doctors and engineers were translated there. Persian and Indian works on medicine and mathematics were added to the Arabic library.

MUSLIM SCHOLARS WROTE ON MANY SUBJECTS

Today scientists are specialists. It is hard to imagine how scientists in Abbassid times could know so many subjects. For example, the famous scholar Ibn Sina wrote books on philosophy, mathematics and astronomy. Ibn Sina's *Encyclopedia of Medicine* has step-by-step descriptions of diseases and cures. Hunayn is famous for his study of the eye. He also led the House of Wisdom, and was a scholar of Greek language. Many Muslim scholars were poets, too. Before automatic printing and recording, people used rhymes to help them remember facts.

Think of Muslim scholars whenever you count. They brought "Arabic numerals" 1-9 from India, and the idea of using zero as a number. Al-Khawarizmi invented Algebra. A scholar from Cairo, Ibn Haitham, solved many problems in optics. Later scientists used his measurements to make lenses for telescopes and microscopes. Muslim scholars tested Greek and Persian ideas on astronomy. They measured the earth and stars with instruments invented in the Khalifahs' royal observatories. Their work helped Muslim scholars to learn navigation and make accurate maps.

Medical doctors are the most famous Muslim scientists in the West. Ibn Sina, Al-Razi, Al-Zahrawi, Ibn-Rushd and many others wrote books used for centuries. European doctors also used them until modern times. They studied anatomy of humans and animals. Surgeons described their instruments, ways to mend broken bones and eye operations. Others wrote encyclopedias about medicines. Rich and poor patients were treated in clean hospitals that had pharmacies for mixing pills, ointments and syrups.

Muslim scholars wrote about agriculture. Farmers developed new and better crops. Muslims introduced many fruits and vegetables to Europe and other lands. Chemistry helped find new ways to mine silver and use other materials.

This scene shows a seaport on the Mediterranean. Muslim merchants traded with Christian, Jewish and other merchants. They loaded the ships with precious goods like spices, coffee, cloth and jewels. On the Mediterranean, the Indian Ocean and in other waters, Muslim traders sailed to many ports. Their work helped build cities and spread Islam. Traders also brought back learning, inventions and fashions from the lands they visited.

74

Architects used mathematics to build and decorate buildings. They designed dams and pumps to control water for farms and cities. Study of history also became important wherever Islam spread. Muslim scholars, both men and women, wrote about many subjects. Many of their books have been lost, and others are found only as translations. From time to time, modern scholars discover copies of their books.

HOW MUSLIM LEARNING SPREAD TO EUROPE

Learning from Baghdad spread throughout the Muslim lands. The art of making paper came from China in the 8th century. Books became cheaper. Educated people wanted many books, and scribes earned a good living in the cities. Merchants carried books and inventions among the lands they visited. Scholars traveled across Muslim lands to meet one another. During the pilgrimage, Muslims brought together ideas from all corners of the world.

Learning spilled over into other lands. Foreign soldiers and merchants noticed the high standard of living in Muslim cities. They brought back goods and ideas to their home countries. Italians were the first Europeans to set up trade with the Muslims. As a result of their contact, Italy was more advanced than the rest of Europe during the Middle Ages. Through Italy came ancient books and new inventions and ways of building. These ideas helped bring a new age to Europe. It is called the **Renaissance**, or rebirth.

Scholars from Christian Europe traveled to study at Muslim universities. Muslims, Christians and Jews lived side-by-side in Al-Andalus (Spain). Customs, fashions, foods and ideas flowed from Muslim Spain to Northern Europe. Translations from Arabic into Latin brought Muslim learning into Europe, often on the backs of donkeys over mountains. Many changes that led to the modern world started from contact with Muslim learning through Spain and Italy.

Understanding Section 3:

1. List the two most important sources of knowledge about Islam, in order.

2. List two ways Muslims preserved the *Qur'an* from changes.

3. Why did Muslim scholars work to set a standard for Islamic laws and practices? On what did they base the standard?

4. Does Islam forbid Muslims to study science? Give reasons for your answer.

5. How did knowledge from other civilizations help science to flower in Muslim lands? Name the civilizations that contributed their knowledge.

6. Write three sentences that describe important contributions of Muslim scientists.

7. List three ways in which knowledge spread from Muslim lands to Europe.

Journey of a Muslim Traveler

In 1325, a Moroccan scholar named Ibn Battuta left his native city of Fez with the pilgrim caravan. He was bound for Makkah, but he became one of the first world travelers. He returned home almost 30 years later. A look at places he visited gives an idea of life in Muslim lands long ago. It shows how Muslims built a civilization that united the Old World.

Traveling across North Africa, Ibn Battuta stopped in Alexandria. Two great harbors handled the Mediterranean traffic. He sailed up the Nile without baggage, since he could get what he needed in **bazaars** (or markets) along the way to Cairo. Cairo was already a huge city. Goods from all over the world filled the city. The skyline was jagged with minarets and domes, seen from the high Citadel where the rulers' palace stood. Ibn Battuta met with other scholars in the mosques and madrasas, which he said "were too many to count." The city's biggest caravansery (a motel for caravans) held 4000 guests. A large hospital provided free treatment to patients.

After visiting Jerusalem's Masjid Al-Aqsa, he caught the annual pilgrim caravan in Damascus. The city's rulers had built beautiful squares and fountains. In the great Umayyad Masjid, Ibn Battuta heard lectures by learned men. He received certificates for his studies.

Makkah was the most international city each year during the pilgrimage. It lay in a desert valley surrounded by bare walls of rock, but Makkah overflowed with fruit from everywhere. Pilgrims bought figs, grapes, lemons, apricots and nuts, as well as watermelons, eggplants and cucumbers. Pilgrims

Ibn Battuta was one of the first world travelers. He started from Fez, Morocco, on his way to make hajj to Makkah. He returned many years later, then set out again. He crossed parts of Asia, the Middle East and Africa by land and sea. At Granada, Spain, he told the story of his travels that we have in a book today.

also traded luxury goods. Muslims of many lands mixed in the streets leading down to the great Haram holding the Kaabah. They prayed side by side. Several times, Ibn Battuta spent a few months studying with scholars at Makkah.

Ibn Battuta went on to Persia and Iraq. He saw Baghdad nearly 100 years after the Mongol attack. It was no longer the Khalifah's capital, but it was still a busy place. In Baghdad, the Silk Road met trade routes from the Indian Ocean and the Persian Gulf. He visited the Persian city of Tabriz, which had the finest bazaar he had ever seen. Under a covered mall with natural air-conditioning, merchants sold goods from all over Europe and Asia.

Returning to Makkah, he sailed from the Red Sea to Yemen. From there, he sailed down the East African coast. In Mogadishu and Mombassa's busy ports, his hosts were dark-skinned scholars and judges. African Muslim merchants traded ivory, rare woods and spices. He saw the stone castle at Kilwa, where African Muslim rulers controlled the gold trade.

Sailing with the **monsoon** (or seasonal wind), he reached port cities in the Persian Gulf. He saw merchants load pearls, jewels, spices and cloth from ships to camel caravans.

From Syria, he sailed in an Italian ship to Turkey. In the royal company of Mongol leader Uzbeg Khan, he rode ox-drawn wagons. Slowly, they moved across the Asian **steppe** (or grassland) to India. The Muslim Mongols protected these trade routes.

He crossed the Himalayan Mountains into the Ganges River valley. Finally, he arrived at Delhi, seat of the Mughal ruler. He was appointed judge and became wealthy. Then he lost his money and nearly his life in palace quarrels. The Sultan appointed him ambassador to China, and he set out again.

East coast ports of India handled Indian Ocean trade. Arabs sailed in swift, triangular-sailed ships. They sailed out and returned with the **monsoons**. They navigated by the stars with **astrolabes**. They used the magnetic **compass,** which they brought to Europe. Ibn Battuta sailed in a five-decked Chinese ship whose captain was Arab.

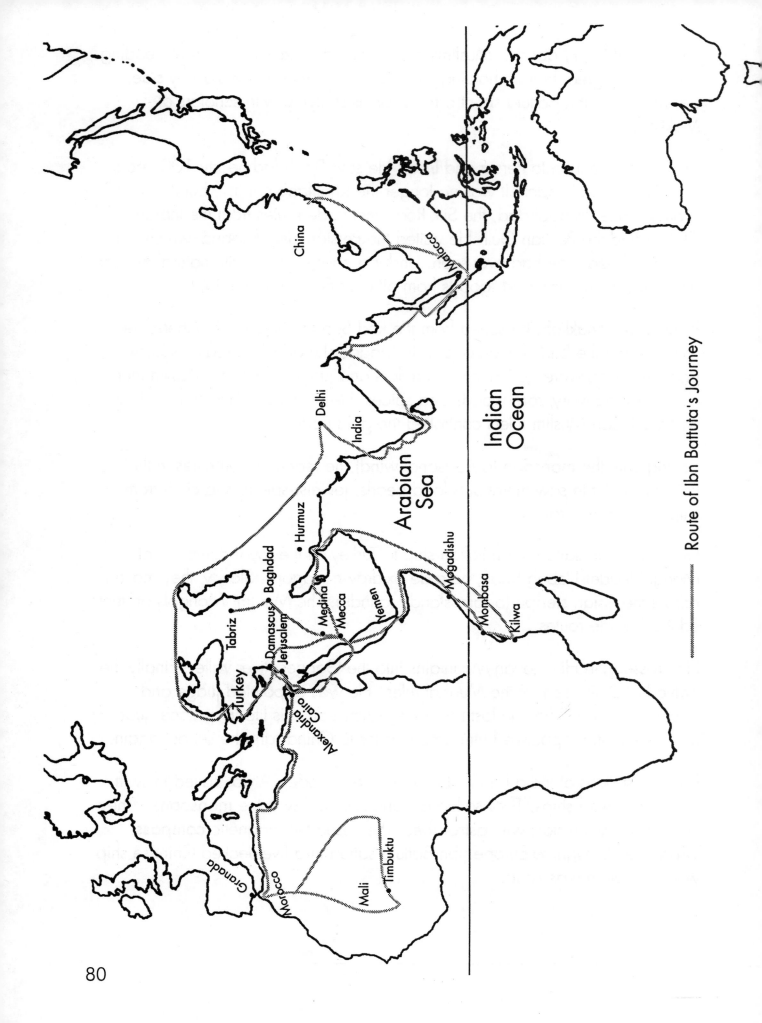

China

Malacca

Delhi

India

Arabian
Sea

Hurmuz

Baghdad

Tabriz

Damascus

Medina

Mecca

Mogadishu

Jerusalem

Yemen

Mombasa

Turkey

Kilwa

Alexandria

Cairo

Indian
Ocean

Granada

Morocco

Mali

Timbuktu

———— Route of Ibn Battuta's Journey

Malacca is a strait where ships enter the China Sea. Even so far from home, Ibn Battuta met other Muslim scholars and religious men. They greeted and spoke in Arabic. They prayed and studied in Arabic. Islam was just then coming to the Spice Islands, welcomed with the trade. It is not known if he reached China or Japan, but other Muslims often did.

After 21 years, he returned home to Morocco. His next stop was the West African land of Mali. This part of Africa supplied about two-thirds of the world's gold. At the end of the Saharan caravan routes, he found the city of Timbuktu, where Islamic learning was honored. Graceful mosques and palaces were built of mud bricks.

Home again, he left for Muslim Spain, where he stayed in the famous Alhambra palace. It still stands today. There Ibn Battuta met the man who helped him write the story of his travels, called the *Rihlah*.

Understanding Section 4:

There are many clues in the *Rihlah* about life during Ibn Battuta's time. See if you can find **evidence** in the story that shows whether the following statements are true or false. **Write T or F, and then list clues from the story that support your answer.**

_____ 1. Citizens of Cairo and other large Muslim cities enjoyed a high standard of living.

_____ 2. Many centuries after the death of Muhammad, Makkah had become a quiet desert town.

_____ 3. Although there were no airplanes or automobiles in those days, many people traveled with ease over long distances.

_____ 4. African countries were very poor at the time when Ibn Battuta visited them.

_____ 5. Bazaars in Ibn Battuta's time were like shopping malls of today.

nomads = tribesmen who live by moving constantly with their grazing animals
oasis, oases = fertile, watered spots in the desert
idols = statues made for worship
pilgrimage = visit to a holy place (in this case, to the Kaabah at Makkah)
pilgrims = people on a pilgrimage
persecute, persecution = to keep people from practicing their faith
diverse = differing or varied
authority = strong and respected leadership
Rennaissance = rebirth of learning and culture in Europe
bazaars = covered markets with many shops
steppe = grassland in Central Asia
monsoon = seasonal winds
astrolabe = tool for navigation by the stars

Words About Islam
Allah = name of the One God in Arabic
Islam = religion of belief in Allah and the prophethood of Muhammad
　　　　(it means "submission" to God's will)
Muslim = believers in Islam (not "Muhammadan")
Qur'an = the holy book of Islam
sunnah = Muhammad's example or way of life
hadith = sayings and deeds of Muhammad
surah = chapter of the Qur'an
hijra = the migration of Muslims from Makkah to Medina
masjid = mosque, or Muslim house of prayer and study
hajj = pilgrimage to the Ka'aba at Makkah

Some Other Arabic Words
Muhajirun = the Migrants from Makkah
Ansar = the Helpers, or Muslims of Medina
jihad = an effort, defending the religion
khalifah = successor to Muhammad's leadership of the Muslims
ilm = knowledge
fiqh = practical guide to Islamic behavior and law
sirah = the history of Muhammad's ﷺ life and community
shari'ah = Islamic law
madrasas = schools or colleges
fitnah = a time of dispute

Part IV:

Teaching Suggestions &
Enrichment Activities

The maps and illustrations that accompany the student text are designed as coloring book pages. They aid comprehension of the visual content by allowing the student to study them in detail. The illustrations provide clues to everyday life that are not included in the text, and may be brought out in classroom discussion as the illustrations are colored. Classes may produce a lasting reminder of their study by coloring the maps and illustrations and covers, reinforcing the cover pages with cardboard or plastic lamination, and binding the booklet with staples, rings or string.

1. Pre-Reading:
a. Using selected verses from the Qur'an, discuss the importance of studying history for Muslims. Ideally, the students could search for such verses as an assignment, using a database or an index to the Qur'an. Have students write a paragraph or essay on the importance of studying the past for Muslims.
b. Using a world wall map, orient the students to the location of lands where Muslims live today. To introduce the subject of Islamic History, brainstorm to see what information and impressions the students hold. Have a secretary list these ideas. During the course of the unit, these ideas can be tested against available information, and a final evaluation made as a concluding activity.

CHAPTER ONE, Section 1:
2. Assuming that the last unit studied was the Roman Empire, review the Western Roman empire after the barbarian invasions, and the Eastern Roman empire, with its capital at Constantinople, which lasted another 1000 years. To lead into the unit's introduction, explain that ancient Rome, Greece, and Egypt traded with Asian, African and Arabian lands. Burn some frankincense crystals or other incense from a Middle East specialty shop. Ask why it was an important product. On a world wall map, orient the students to places mentioned in the text, trace the ancient Arabian trade route. List other products which may have travelled on it [silk from China, cotton from India, spices, jewels, pearls, etc].

3. To illustrate the concept of **nomadism**, have the students draw a desert scene. Comparing impressions, discuss possibilities for life in the desert, how large a group could survive together, and what their diet, homes and clothing would consist of. Proceeding from desert vegetation, discuss why staying in one place to farm or raise animals would be impossible. Speculate how much land a tribe might need and what kind of conflict might arise with other tribes. What sort of entertainment might be available to people who must carry all their possessions with them? Then draw an oasis, and follow a similar line of discussion. Alternatively, have the class view slides or photos of desert and oasis.

4. Review the story of Makkah. Connecting with themes of nomadism and caravan trade, discuss how cities grow and develop where conditions are right. Note that Abraham is recognized as a prophet by Jews, Christians and Muslims. This theme will be picked up later. Students may expand on the story of Ibrahim, Hajjar, Ismael and the founding of Makkah, since it is relevant to Islamic rites of pilgrimage. Topics for discussion include concepts of tradition, change and idol-worship (why statues and objects have been worshipped, and where this continues today). Additional reading for students includes *The Prophets* (Syed Ali Ashraf, UMO National Muslim Council of U.K., 1980) and *Children's Series:Stories of Some Prophets* (A.S. Hashim).

CHAPTER ONE, Section 2:

NOTE: The sketch of Muhammad's life and the story of the early Muslim community is intended as an outline. The goal of this unit is to place the events of Muhammad's life and his prophethood in historical perspective. An exhaustive study of the Sirah would include a great deal more detail, and may certainly be undertaken in conjunction with this unit where time permits. It is recommended to combine this unit with such a cross-disciplinary unit on the Sirah Nabawiyah in Islamic Studies. Where this is not possible, it is suggested that students do outside readings on the Sirah from recommmended readings, bringing the extra information into class discussions. Two such sources are *The Life of the Prophet Muhammad S.A.W.* (Safa Khulusi, UMO National Muslim Council of U.K., 1985), *Children's Series: Life of Muhammad*, (A.S. Hashim), *Muhammad the Great Prophet* (Iqbal Ahmad Azami), *Muhammad the Last Messenger* (Alia N. Athar) and *Stories of the Sirah* (Tasneemah and Abidullah Ghazi, IQRA Foundation).

1. Review the outline of Muhammad's biography. Explain that membership in tribe and family was extremely important in his culture. Not only the immediate family was important, but also the family in the past. Arabs kept long lists of their geneology, or tribal ancestors, in memory. Muhammad ﷺ was born into a noble family; Abd Al-Muttalib was highly respected as one of the chiefs of the tribe. It was clear that he enjoyed special favor from Allah, since he was chosen to find the treasure and Zamzam. Abu Talib, though not wealthy, was also influential, and later offered protection to Muhammad ﷺ, though he did not accept Islam. Being an orphan was a great disadvantage in a tribal system. People not attached to one of the important tribes could expect no protection unless they were adopted as "clients" of a tribe. Explain how this relates to the discussion on desert survival and nomadism. (Survival depended upon the group, and the group depended upon its traditional rights to certain grazing lands. It would be very difficult to survive without the family.)

CHAPTER ONE, Section 3:

1. As a pre-reading activity, have the students write about time they like to spend alone, favorite places for it, and things they sometimes think about. Discuss Muhammad's retreat from everyday life and his reasons for seeking solitude. To expand on the con-

cept of prophethood, you may wish to elaborate on the stories of prophets both within and outside the Judeo-Christian-Islamic tradition. Make a working definition of prophethood, its purpose according to different belief systems. Discuss the story and the content of the first message, the first five verses of Surat 'Iqra. For additional information and reading, see bibliography.

Define and discuss persecution. Ask why certain members of Muhammad's tribe may have accepted him readily and why the chiefs resisted. Challenge the students to give reasons for taking agressive measures against individuals or groups because of their beliefs. Identify and analyse examples of persecution from history. They may be reminded of persecution of Christians by the Romans, or of persecution during the days of political/religious struggle in the Byzantine Empire. Most familiar to the students may be religious persecution of various Christian groups in Europe which led to the pilgrims' settlement of Plymouth, Massachusetts and other colonies. Discuss religious persecution in today's world, the forms it takes, its purposes, and specific incidents.

CHAPTER ONE, Section 4:

1. Review events leading to migration of the Muslims, and finally Muhammad ﷺ, to Medina. Why could they no longer continue living in Makkah? [For more detail on the actual migration, see bibliography.] Discuss the task which faced Muhammad ﷺ as leader of the community at Medina. Explain that various tribes resided there, not all of whom were Muslim. It was important for Muhammad ﷺ to reorganize the community and establish it on a new basis of brotherhood, cooperation and tolerance. This meant that the tribe would become less important — a revolutionary change in their thinking. The partnership or brotherhood between Ansar and Muhajirun is significant for these reasons, in addition to material assistance for the impoverished migrants.

2. The community at Medina provides an opportunity to discuss citizenship and law. Have the students contribute to a chart on posterboard. Using any practical format, (1) generate a list of requirements for a prosperous, peaceful community. (2) List areas of community life which require cooperation and rules to keep order and justice (examples: family life, marriage, inheritance; buying and selling; work and workers; crime and other harmful things; relations with outside communities) (3) Write a list of laws which would cover the areas in the second part and bring about conditions listed in the first category. In this light, discuss the Islamic concept of building a society based on a unified system of personal, social and public rules. (For follow-up and extension of this activity, see Activity # 2, Chapter 2, Section 2.)

3. Discuss traditions and how they arise. Why are deep-rooted traditions so difficult to change, even when they no longer fulfill a constructive purpose? Discuss some traditions or customs to which people cling. What forces can make them change? Why

was Muhammad's community willing and able to change rapidly? Do we have some traditions or customs today which are not healthy in the Islamic view?

4. Students may be assigned reports or projects on specific battles and campaigns. Not all are named or discussed in the text; each has fascinating stories of the companions and events which will interest the students. Review the sequence of conflict between the Muslims and their adversaries of Quraysh. [For more detail on individual episodes of the conflict, see bibliography.] Some students may be interested in military history and making models of battlefield layouts special reports. Discuss why the Muslims wanted a treaty and why Quraysh resisted. Explain that when the treaty was finally made, its terms seemed to favor Quraysh so much that the Muslims were amazed that Muhammad 🕮 had agreed to it. But events bore him out, since it forced Quraysh to recognize the Muslims as a group to contend with, gave them legitimacy, and allowed the message to spread freely. Discuss why Muhammad 🕮 granted Quraysh pardon after years of battle and persecution.

5 Play a game to identify the sequence of famous battles, the year in which they took place, and other facts. One possible game is "Concentration," in which facts or names of battles or persons are written on cards and arranged in a square of 9, 16 or 25 cards. The cards are then covered with numbered cards. The leader or teacher reads identifying information, and the students search, at random at first, for the matching information by calling out numbers and having an assistant uncover the card until the match is found. Once it is found, the card is left uncovered; if the match is incorrect, the card is covered again. The game continues until all the cards have been uncovered. This activity may also be used to review information on the spread of Islam, important battles and scientific contributions in Chapter 2.

CHAPTER TWO, Section 1:
1. **Pre-reading:**
a. Call attention to the fact that the guiding theme of this chapter is to see how Muslims lived up to and applied the example set by Prophet Muhammad 🕮. As they read Chapter 2, students may keep a chart with two columns, recording in column #1 what they feel are positive achievements of Muslim civilization and recording in column #2 negative actions and trends.
b. Using the map on p. 50 of the text and a classroom map, orient the students to the area under Islam after Muhammad's death. Identify and characterize surrounding lands (Byzantium, Persia, Egypt, etc.) by reviewing information from past units. Identify geographic barriers which surround the Arabian Peninsula.

2. Review **persecution**. Discuss the Arabic word **jihad**, its significance as inner struggle to achieve personal goals and as regrettably necessary action to counter persecution. List Islamic controls on military action and compare these with some points from the Geneva Accords. Discussion may arrive at the subject of terrorism. Islamic restrictions

on any type of military action represent a clear condemnation of terrorism. [Terrorism is not an invention of self-styled "Muslims," but an ancient tactic. The term "holy war" is also not unique to Islam. Clearly stated standards for warfare were not achieved elsewhere until the Geneva Accords.]

NOTE Since the word **jihad** has entered popular vocabulary in connection with Middle East conflict, it is important to clarify its proper meaning and context in Islam. The role of military conquest in the spread of Islam has been misunderstood and misrepresented. In light of historical events, it is illogical to maintain that the bulk of conversions to Islam took place under threat of death. First, vast lands converted by force would hardly have remained docile enough to be controlled by a minority group of Arabs. Second, such conversions would hardly have been lasting or deep enough to produce a cultural flowering. Third, the theory of conversion by force does not explain historical evidence like the continuous presence of Christian sects which suffered persecution under the Byzantines, of the Coptic Church in Egypt, and the continuous presence of Sephardic Jews in the Middle East throughout Islamic history. It is well known in Jewish scholarship that Judaism experienced a flowering after Islamic rule ended the insecurity of persecution under Persians, Romans and Byzantines. The principle of religious tolerance is firmly rooted in Qur'anic doctrine and Muslim practice. Isolated exceptions should not be mistaken for the rule. [For further reseach on this topic, see bibliography.]

3. At this time you may wish to view the filmstrip set, part 1, "The Spread of Islam," which adds more detail for reinforcement and enrichment.

4. Ask the students to list ways in which civilizations come in contact with each other. Have them visualize journeys, conversations, sightseeing, and other activities which bring about influence among different cultures. What things (influences) can convince a person to adopt another's way of life, ideas, inventions, and religion? List these factors.

5. Using the map on p.52 and a wall map, trace the expansion of the Muslim lands; compare these with countries in the modern world, identifying lands with contemporary Muslim populations.

CHAPTER TWO, Section 2:

1. Continue Activity #5, Chapter 2, Section 1, using physical relief, vegetation and climate maps to explore geographic features of the expanded state. Recall civilizations, languages, and religions on these lands. Mention outcomes of other unifying conquests (Alexander, the Romans, etc.) to explain cultural layering.

2. Return to Activity #4, Chapter 1, Section 4. Review chart on community government. Add posterboard, extending the chart to include government of a large state. Discuss challenges and obstacles, and some means for joining lands under just rule.

At this time you may wish to have the students role play through "point of view" writing project on Worksheet # 5.

3.   Identify Muslim ruling groups and place in chronological order. [Students may want to play another round of "Concentration."] In analysing their achievements and changes in the nature and style of rule, discuss conclusions from the previous activity. Analysis is limited by the amount of information which can be presented at this level. The text presents a brief summary of the tone and some achievements by each group. Time permitting, the teacher may wish to supplement this information through his/her own research or student reports on individual rulers or ruling groups. Children's literature on these topics includes *The Rightly-Guided Khalifs* (Safa Khulusi and S. Al-Dabbagh), *Al-Khulafah Al-Rashidun* (A. S. Hashim), *Devoted Companions* (A.S. Hashim), *The Heroes of Islam Series* (Prof. Fazl Ahmad), *The Muslim Heroes Series* (Mahmoud Esmail Sieny), and *Umar Bin Abdul Aziz* (S. Zakir Aijaz).

CHAPTER TWO, Section 3:

1.   It is important to have the students clarify the process by which the Qur'an and the Hadith came to be set down in writing. Particularly impressive is the fact that its transmission over the generations has been secured by a double mode: it was memorized and recited under careful conditions, and it was transmitted as a written document from the beginning. The Hadith literature was similarly collected. It is interesting that the Qur'an was transmitted by means of the highest grade of transmission, namely, by a large number of people in the first generation, to a large number in the second, and so on. By contrast, the lowest grade involves transmission of a text from only one person in the first generation through a single chain of persons.

    As part of the discussion, students should be introduced to the development by early Muslims of a system for transmitting information about the Qur'an, Arabic language, the Sirah and Islamic history. For the teacher's information, the book by A.A. Duri, listed in the reference section, is very useful; Chapter 1 describes Muslim scholarly activity in the first three centuries.

    Finally, students should note the way in which the collected information was systematized and developed into the branches of the religious sciences.
    NOTE To bring the discussion to modern times, have the students compare and contrast modern methods for verifying history and people's words with techniques available in the early history of Islam.

2.   A major theme of Islamic history is the dialogue between high ideals and Islamic principles and Muslim leaders' attempts to implement or avoid them. This dialogue is reflected in the title of Marshall G.S. Hodgson's *The Venture of Islam: History and Conscience in a World Civilization*. To bring this concept closer to the students' experience, it may be useful to present the parallel case of the United States' ongoing attempt to implement the high ideals of its Constitution for comparison and contrast. Referring to the early community at Medina, and the first four Khalifahs, explain why

The Qur'an and Muhammad's example have the force of law for Muslims. Efforts of scholars mentioned at the end of Section 2 were similar to those of the Constitution's framers and Supreme Court justices, though they were working largely outside of official auspices, and often in some type of opposition. Many of the principles embodied in the U.S. Constitution have parallels in Islamic law. In many respects, of course, Islamic Shari'ah has yet to be fully implemented in time and space.

NOTE This is an excellent time to revisit the discussion on the uses of the study of history among Muslims. Islam teaches that the value and importance of historical study is to take the measure of the past, to see what became of people who lived before our time. It is of the utmost importance to the development of Islamic values and character that a balance be achieved between extolling the virtues of Muslim civilization and honest criticism of Muslims' failings. One of the most difficult tasks for students of history is evaluation of the extent to which the scholarly tradition influenced Muslim states at various times. [For further information, see bibliography.]

3. ART PROJECT/ART HISTORY: Show examples of Arabic calligraphy and geometric designs from books on Muslim art. Explain that Muslims refined the art of calligraphy for two reasons: first, Muslims honor the Qur'an as the word of Allah and like to decorate public and private spaces with inspirational verses. Second, Islamic principles forbid or strongly discourage representation of animate creatures. Calligraphic, geometric and arabesque designs were raised to a high art in Muslim civilization. Have the students experiment with combining letters into shapes and designs and/or learning some techniques of fancy lettering and illumination. Either English or Arabic alphabets could be used.

4. At this time you may wish to view the filmstrip "Muslim Science and Scholarship" for reinforcement and additional detail. For further exploration of the topic, the students may enjoy the skills activities on Worksheets #3 and #4, "Words from Arabic" and "Arabic Numerals."

5. ART PROJECT/ HISTORY OF TECHNOLOGY: Students enjoy making paper. The process combines scientific, historical and artistic dimensions. Most art teachers have expertise in specific techniques. How-To books show simple techniques for making paper. Museums have exhibits and demonstrations on papermaking, bookbinding, etc. **If a project is not possible, show samples of parchment and various types of paper (perhaps also Egyptian papyrus, which was widely used in the Middle East long after the Pharoahs) from an art store. Discuss the technique and its origins in China, as well as the enormous importance of this invention for the spread of ideas and commerce.

6. Review discussion from Activity #4, Chapter 2, Section 1 on cultural influence and contact among civilizations as a pre- activity for viewing the filmstrip "Muslim Influence in Europe."

CHAPTER TWO, Section 4:

1. This section introduces some skills needed for working with primary source material. Rather than quoting from the original, we preferred to sacrifice directness for a broader view of Ibn Battuta's world. The exercise printed in the text at the end of the section requires explanation of the term evidence (see KEY) so that students understand the task. It is intended to build reading comprehension and inference skills which can be applied in later units to actual primary source material.

2. To orient the students to trade routes which will be useful for later discussion of Europe's Age of Exploration, use the map on p.47. You may also wish to have the students do Worksheet #3, "Arabic Words in English," since many of the words are related to amenities of urban life.

Concluding Activities:

1. Use Worksheet #1, "Crossword Fun," and #6, "Time Line," for review. A file of test questions in various formats is provided for each chapter. Evaluation is recommended at the conclusion of Chapter One, after Sections 1 and 2 of Chapter Two, and at the conclusion of the unit.

2. Suggestions for final evaluation include a writing activity, roundtable discussion, current events or other project which would compare the students' impressions listed at the start of the unit with information gleaned through the study. (See Activity #1, Chapter 1, Section 1.)

3. A test question file is included with the unit. If the students have shared individual research with the class, it may be desirable to include extra credit questions on this research, or to hold the students responsible for a portion of the information from these reports or projects which was emphasized in class discussion. It is important to reinforce in the students' minds that the teacher is not the only source of information.

Books:

Al-Mas'udi and His World. Ahmad M.H. Shboul. London: Ithaca Press, 1979.

Arab Administration. S. A. Q. Husaini. Delhi: Idarah-I Adabiyat-I Delli, 1949.

The Adventures of Ibn Battuta. Ross E. Dunn, Berkeley & Los Angeles: University of California Press, 1986.

The Arab Navigation. Syed Sulaiman Nadvi. Lahore: Sh. Muhammad Ashraf, 1966.

Arabic Writing and Arab Libraries. S. M. Imamuddin. London: Ta Ha Publishers, 1983.

The Cultural Atlas of Islam. Ismail R. Al Faruqi and Lois L. Al Faruqi. New York: Macmillan Publishing Co., 1986.

Decisive Battles of Islam. Amir Hasan Siddiqi. Kuwait: Islamic Book Publishers, 1986.

The End of the Jihad State. Khalid Yahya Blankinship. Albany: State University of New York Press, 1994.

The Genius of Arab Civilization. J. R. Hayes, ed.. London: Eurabia Publishing Ltd., 1983.

A History of Islamic Law. N. J. Coulson. Edinburgh: Edinburgh University Press, 1964.

A History of Islamic Spain. W. Montgomery Watt and Pierre Cachia. Edinburgh: Edinburgh University Press, 1965.

A History of Islam in West Africa. J. S. Trimingham. Oxford: Oxford University Press, 1962.

A History of the Arab Peoples. Albert Hourani. Cambridge: Harvard University Press, 1991.

Islamic History: a New Interpretation. M. A. Shaban. Cambridge: Cambridge University Press, 1971.

Islamic Surveys: The Influence of Islam on Medieval Europe. W. Mongomery Watt. Edinburgh: Edinburgh University Press, 1972.

The Life of Muhammad. Muhammad Haykal (I. R. Al Faruqi, trans.). Indianapolis: American Trust Publications, 1976.

Medieval Islam. Dominique Sourdel. London: Routledge & Kegan Paul, 1979.

Moorish Spain. Richard Fletcher. New York: Henry Holt & Company, 1992.

Muhammad: His Life Based on the Earliest Sources. Martin Lings. Rochester, VT: Inner Traditions, 1983.

Muslim Contribution to Geography. Nafis Ahmad. Delhi: Adam Publishers, 1945, 1982.

On the Political System of the Islamic State. Muhammad S. El-Awa. Indianapolis: American Trust Publications, 1980.

The Oxford History of the Classical World. John Boardman, et al., eds. Oxford: Oxford University Press: 1986.

The Oxford Illustrated History of Medieval Europe. George Holmes, ed. Oxford: Oxford University Press, 1988.

The Rise of Historical Writing Among the Arabs. A. A. Duri (transl. L. I. Conrad). Princeton: Princeton University Press, 1983.

Storm from the East. Robert Marshall. Berkeley: University of California Press, 1993.(with TV series)

The Venture of Islam: History and Conscience in a World Civilization. Vols. 1-3. Marshall G. S. Hodgson. Chicago: University of Chicago Press, 1974.

Articles:

"Arabia's Frankincense Trail," T. J. Abercrombie, *National Geographic*, Vol. 168, No. 4, October 1985.

"Damascus" and other features, *Ahlan Wasahlan* (Saudi Arabian Airlines Magazine), Vol. 7, Issue 7, October 1983.

"Ibn Battuta: Prince of Travelers," T. J. Abercrombie, *National Geographic*, Vol. 180, No. 6, December 1991.

"Science: the Islamic Legacy," *Aramco World Magazine*. Special World's Fair Edition. New York: Aramco Corporation.

"Suleyman the Magnificent," Merle Severy, *National Geographic*, Vol. 172, No. 5, November, 1987.

"The Middle East and the Age of Discovery," Paul Lunde, *Aramco World Magazine*, Vol. 43, No. 3 (May-June 1992).

Other Sources:

The Alim Islamic Study Software. (Computer Databases on Qur'an, Hadith, Fiqh, Biographies, Islamic History). I.S.L. Software Corporation, P.O. Box 90005, Houston, TX 77290.

Fiqh Al-Sunnah. Sayyid Sabiq. Cairo: Dar Al-Turath Al-Araby, 1958.

The Holy Qur'an: English Translation of the Meanings and Commentary. Revised and Edited by The Presidency of Islamic Researches, IFTA, Call and Guidance. Madinah: King Fahd Holy Qur'an Printing Complex, 1410 H.

The Meaning of the Glorious Qur'an. Marmaduke Pickthall. Makkah: Muslim World League, 1977.

The Day the Universe Changed. James Burke. TV Documentary Series.

CHAPTER ONE

Section 1:

1. What important product was carried by caravans through Arabia in ancient times?
2. How did the desert tribes survive in the harsh land of Arabia? What personal qualities did they need to have?
3. For what purpose did Ibrahim build the Ka'aba, and how did later generations change the Ka'aba?
4. What caused Makkah to grow and become a city?

Key

1. Incense was carried from Yemen through Arabia by caravan.
2. Desert tribes moved constantly with their animals among oases. They had to be loyal, generous and skilled and courageous in fighting.
3. He built it for worship of One God, and later generations filled the house with idols.
4. Many people came to visit the Ka'aba each year, and its water supply helped it become a caravan stop and trade center.

Section 2:

1. What was the name of Muhammad's tribe and where was he born?
2. Describe Muhammad's family situation as a child.
3. As a young man, what was his position in his tribe?
4. Who was Khadijah?

Key

1. He was born at Makkah into the tribe of Quraysh.
2. He became an orphan at the age of six, and lived with his grandfather, and later with his uncle.
3. Muhammad ﷺ was respected as an honest, wise man and a peacemaker.
4. Khadijah was a rich widow and caravan trader who asked Muhammad (pbuh) to marry her.

Section 3:

1. Why did Muhammad ﷺ visit the cave at Hira' each year?
2. What happened to Muhammad ﷺ in the cave that frightened him?
3. What is a prophet? What other prophets do Muslims also believe in?
4. Did Muhammad's family and tribe accept him as a prophet?
5. What did the leaders of Makkah do when the Muslims began to increase in number?
6. Who offered to help the Muslims? Where did Muhammad ﷺ send the Muslims?

Key
1. He wanted to think deeply about man's place in the world and get away from every-day life.
2. He told that an angel came to him and told him to recite words from Allah.
3. A prophet is a person who receives messages from Allah. Muslims also believe in Ibrahim (Abraham), Musa (Moses), Issa (Jesus) and many others.
4. His family and household accepted him, but most of his tribe did not.
5. They were persecuted, or made to suffer for their beliefs. They also tried to make Muhammad stop teaching.
6. People from the city of Yathrib offered Muhammad protection. He sent Muslims to live in Yathrib.

Section 4:
1. What event marks the beginnning of the Muslim calendar? What is the date according to the Christian calendar?
2. In what way did the Muslims' situation improve at Medina?
3. Name the two groups in Medina who formed a brotherhood and what do their names mean?
4. Name the message which Muslims honor as Allah's word. How long did it take to complete the Qur'an?
5. List two laws of the Muslim community which came from the Qur'an.
6. Name two big changes which Islam brought to the Muslims' way of life.
7. Tell what each side, Quraysh and the Muslims, wanted to do that brought them to the point of war. Why?
8. What victory did the Muslims win without fighting? What did Muhammad do after he entered the city?
9. How far had Islam spread by the end of Muhammad's life?

Key
1. Muhammad's migration, or Hijra, to Yathrib (Medina) in 622 C.E. marks the beginning of the Muslim calendar.
2. They were able to practice Islam without persecution, and they began to build their community.
3. Muhajirun (migrants) and Ansar (helpers) formed a brotherhood.
4. The message is called the Qur'an, and it took 23 years to complete.
5. Answers vary.
6. Women were given rights; drinking wine and gambling were forbidden.
7. Quraysh wanted to stop the Muslims because they threatened their powerful position. The Muslims wanted a treaty so that they could spread the message of Islam without fear of attack.
8. An army of 10,000 Muslims entered Makkah without fighting. He forgave Quraysh and cleaned the idols out of the Ka'aba.
9. Most of the tribes in Arabia were Muslim, and letters had been sent to kings in the great empires.

CHAPTER TWO

Section 1:

1. Give an example of religious persecution long ago.
2. Why did Islam permit fighting?
3. Why did Muhammad place strict conditions on the Muslim armies?
4. List several reasons why the Persian and Byzantine Empires were weak.
5. From each of the following pairs, choose the land which came under Islamic rule first:
a. Palestine —— Persia
b. India —— Egypt
c. Southern France —— North Africa
6. How long did the Muslims rule Spain? For extra credit, what other historical event happened in 1492?
7. Name three ways by which Islam spread to other lands.

Key

1. Answers vary.
2. Fighting was only allowed to defend against persecution.
3. He wanted to protect innocent people from harm and injustice, and he did not want the Muslims to fight for goods and land.
4. They had fought each other for a long time, they had spent much money in taxes, and their citizens were tired of war and persecution.
5. Palestine/Egypt/North Africa
6. Muslims ruled Spain for 700 years. Columbus discovered the Americas in 1492.
7. Answers vary (trade, books, migration, etc.)

Section 2:

1. List two problems faced by the rulers of the Muslim lands.
2. Why were Arabs the first rulers of the Muslim state?
3. What name was given to the first four Khalifahs, or successors to Muhammad's leadership? Why?
4. How is the ruler chosen in a <u>dynasty</u> and how is it different from the way the first four Khalifahs were chosen?
5. In what ways were the Umayyad and Abbassid Dynasties different from the early Khalifahs?
6. Which two groups of skilled soldiers from Central Asia accepted Islam and ruled over Muslim territories?
7. What was the name for the Mongol rulers in India?
8. What Muslim ruling group renamed Constantinople in 1458, and ruled until the 20th century?
9. Why did the Muslim scholars work to set a standard for Islamic laws and practices? On what did they base the standard?

Key

1. The lands had expanded to a large size very quickly, and those lands were very diverse in geography, culture, etc.
2. The Arabs were most familiar with Islamic laws and beliefs.
3. The first four Khalifahs were called "Rightly Guided," because they lived simply and ruled wisely, following Qur'an and Muhammad's example.
4. In a dynasty, a ruler choses his son or other family member to follow him. The former Khalifahs had been chosen by the community from its best leaders.
5. Answers vary. They lived in palaces like kings;they were more distant from the people whom they ruled; they had many officials, etc.
6. Seljuk Turks and Mongols both became Muslim ruling groups.
7. The Mongol rulers in India were called Mughals.
8. The Ottomans renamed it "Islanbul" and ruled until the 20th century.
9. They wanted the people to hold their leaders up to high standards. They based the standard on ilm, or knowledge.

Section 3:

1. List the two most important sources of knowledge about Islam, in order.
2. List two things which Muslims did to preserve the Qur'an from changes.
3. Does Islam forbid Muslims to study science? Give reasons for your answer.
4. How did knowledge from other civilizations help science to flower in Muslim lands? Name the civilizations which contributed their knowledge.
5. Write three sentences which describe important contributions of Muslim scientists.
6. List three ways in which scientific knowledge and ideas spread from Muslim lands to Europe.

Key

1. The two most important sources are the Qur'an and the Sunnah, or example of Muhammad.
2. Answers vary. They memorized it while Muhammad was living; they collected it and wrote it down; they improved the system of writing Arabic, etc.
3. No, the Qur'an and Muhammad told the Muslims to seek knowledge about the natural world.
4. Knowledge from Persian, Greek, Roman, Indian and Chinese civilization was translated in the Muslim lands.
5. Answers vary.
6. Answers vary. Paper made books cheaper, so many people wanted them; merchants carried goods and ideas to other lands; scholars travelled to study in Muslim lands; books by Muslims were translated; [Italy and Spain were points of contact].

Section 4:

There are many clues in the Rihlah about life during Ibn Battuta's time. See if you can find evidence in the story that shows whether the following statements are true or false. Write T or F, and then list clues from the story which support your answer.

____ 1. Citizens of Cairo and other large Muslim cities enjoyed a high standard of living.

____ 2. Many centuries after the death of Muhammad ﷺ, Makkah had become a quiet desert town.

____ 3. Although there were no airplanes or automobiles in those days, many people travelled with ease over long distances.

____ 4. African countries were very poor at the time when Ibn Battuta visited them.

____ 5. Bazaars in Ibn Battuta's time were like shopping malls of today.

Key

Thoroughly explain this inference skills activity before beginning. The students may require definition of evidence and discussion on how to use "primary sources" to gather it. Answers will vary.

1. <u>True</u> — Cairo was very large and had many tall buildings; there were hotels, hospitals and schools; cities had planned squares with fountains; citizens could buy many goods.

2. <u>False</u> — During the pilgrimage each year, Makkah was host to Muslims from many lands; pilgrims brought many goods to trade; although it was a desert town, its markets were full of all kinds of fruits and vegetables.

3. <u>True</u> — Many scholars and merchants travelled regularly; ships used compasses and astrolabes to travel as far as China; goods travelled over very long distances; there were hotels and caravanseries for travellers.

4. <u>False</u> — Ibn Battuta described African Muslim merchants in gold and other goods in East Africa; Mali supplied two-thirds of the world's gold then; Africans had busy ports and cities with castles and palaces.

5. <u>True</u> — The bazaar at Tabriz was covered and air-conditioned like our malls; a customer could buy everything he needed at a bazaar; bazaars offered rich goods from many lands for sale.

Chapter 1
Multiple choice

1. b
2. c
3. c
4. a
5. b
6. c

Who's Who and What?

e - Abraham
h - Yemen
f - Quraysh
b - Khadijah
g - Muslim
a - Allah
d - Muhajirun
c - Ansar

Thinking Questions (Answers vary. See text under Ch. 1 and Ch 2.)

Chronological Ordering

1. Muhammad ﷺ migrates to Medinah.
2. Muhammad ﷺ cleans idols out of the Kaabah.
3. Rightly-Guided Khalifahs rule for 30 years.
4. The Persian Empire falls to the Muslims.
5. Umayyad family rules Muslim lands.
6. Islam spread to China and Spain.

Basic Understandings About Islam

One; Allah; Arabic; submits to; Qur'an; Muhammad ﷺ; Sunnah; Moses, Jesus, Abraham, (etc.)

Science in Muslim Civilization

Answers may list names or specific contributions cited in text or video.
Mathematics: Al-Khwarizmi, Ibn Haitham, Al-Tusi, Ibn Sina
Medicine: Ibn Sina, Al-Zahrawi, Al-Razi, Ibn Rushd, Hunayn, surgery,
Astronomy: Ibn Sina, Al-Biruni
Geography: Al-Masudi, Al-Biruni, Al-Idrisi
Navigation: compass, astrolabe, maps, Ibn Majid, Sulaiman Tajir

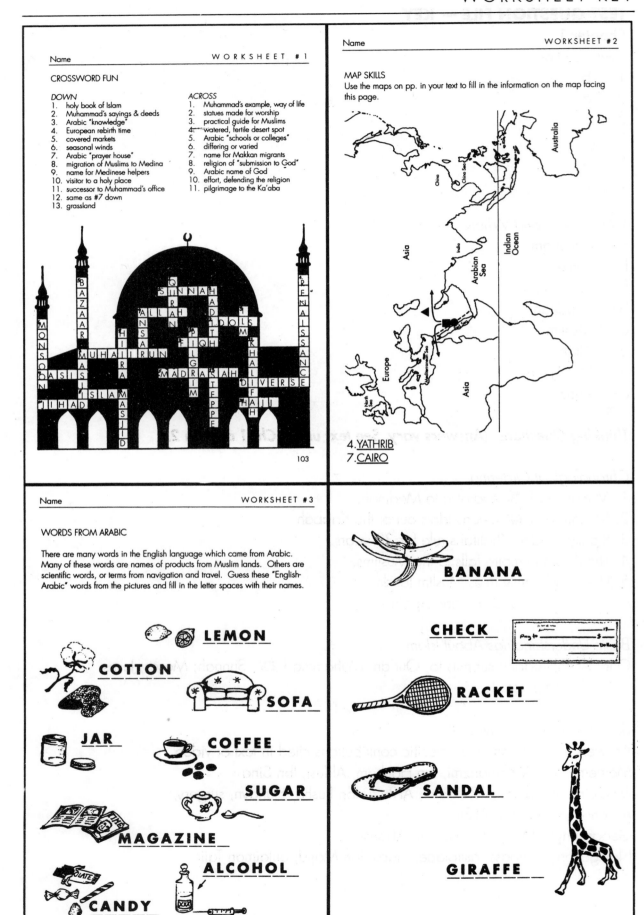

Name _____   WORKSHEET #1

CROSSWORD FUN

DOWN
1. holy book of Islam
2. Muhammad's sayings & deeds
3. Arabic "knowledge"
4. European rebirth time
5. covered markets
6. seasonal winds
7. Arabic "prayer house"
8. migration of Muslims to Medina
9. name for Medinese helpers
10. visitor to a holy place
11. successor to Muhammad's office
12. same as #7 down
13. grassland

ACROSS
1. Muhammad's example, way of life
2. statues made for worship
3. practical guide for Muslims
4. watered, fertile desert spot
5. Arabic "schools or colleges"
6. differing or varied
7. name for Makkan migrants
8. religion of "submission to God"
9. Arabic name of God
10. effort, defending the religion
11. pilgrimage to the Ka'aba

103

Name _____   WORKSHEET #2

MAP SKILLS
Use the maps on pp. in your text to fill in the information on the map facing this page.

4. YATHRIB
7. CAIRO

Name _____   WORKSHEET #3

WORDS FROM ARABIC

There are many words in the English language which came from Arabic. Many of these words are names of products from Muslim lands. Others are scientific words, or terms from navigation and travel. Guess these "English-Arabic" words from the pictures and fill in the letter spaces with their names.

LEMON

COTTON

SOFA

JAR

COFFEE

SUGAR

MAGAZINE

ALCOHOL

CANDY

BANANA

CHECK

RACKET

SANDAL

GIRAFFE

WORKSHEET KEY

Name _____   WORKSHEET # 4

ARABIC NUMERALS

The number signs you use every day are called "Arabic numerals." The idea of using a separate symbol for each number from 1 to 9 was brought by Muslims from India in the 900s. Before these Arabic numerals came to Europe, Roman numerals were used. To find out which symbols are easier to use, practice using them by answering the questions below. By reading the numerals on the clocks below, you can figure out which number is which.

(Clock with Roman Numerals)   (Clock with Arabic Numerals)

1. Write the symbol for three in Roman **III** and Arabic **٣** numerals.
2. Write the number twelve in Roman **XII** and Arabic **١٢** numerals.
3. How do you think the number 15 is written?
   in Roman numerals **XV** in Arabic numerals **10**

The idea of using zero (0) to hold empty places in 10s, 100s and so on, was also brought by Muslims from India.

4. Write the number ten in Arabic numerals. **1•**
   What symbol is used for zero? **•**
5. Try writing these numbers in Arabic numerals:
   One hundred **1••**   Forty-five **٤٥**
   Can you do it in Roman numerals?

Modern Arabic numerals, above, are different from those that first came from Arabs. Those were like ours today. Arabic numerals are easy to use in arithmetic problems. Try solving these, using the clock above to help you remember the number which stands for each symbol.

LXVII	LXXXII	49177	935629
+ CLIX	+ MCCXIV	+ 1072311	+ 121436
CCXXI	**MCCLIVVI**	**1121488**	**1057065**

113

TIME LINE FOR MUSLIM HISTORY

Time line for Muslim History:
- a. Muhammad was born. — 570
- b. Muhammad migrated to Medina.
- c. Rightly-Guided Khalifahs rule. — 622
- d. Umayyads rule. — 711
- e. Muslim lands stretch from Atlantic Ocean to China. — 750
- f. Abbasids rule. — 1258
- g. Muslim rule in Spain. — 1492
- Mongol armies attack Baghdad.
- Columbus sails to America.

101

Part V:

Unit Activities

CROSSWORD FUN

DOWN
1. holy book of Islam
2. Muhammad's sayings & deeds
3. Arabic "knowledge"
4. European rebirth time
5. covered markets
6. seasonal winds
7. Arabic "prayer house"
8. migration of Muslims to Medina
9. name for Medinese helpers
10. visitor to a holy place
11. successor to Muhammad's office
12. same as #7 down
13. grassland

ACROSS
1. Muhammad's example, way of life
2. statues made for worship
3. practical guide for Muslims
4. watered, fertile desert spot
5. Arabic "schools or colleges"
6. differing or varied
7. name for Makkan migrants
8. religion of "submission to God"
9. Arabic name of God
10. effort, defending the religion
11. pilgrimage to the Ka'aba

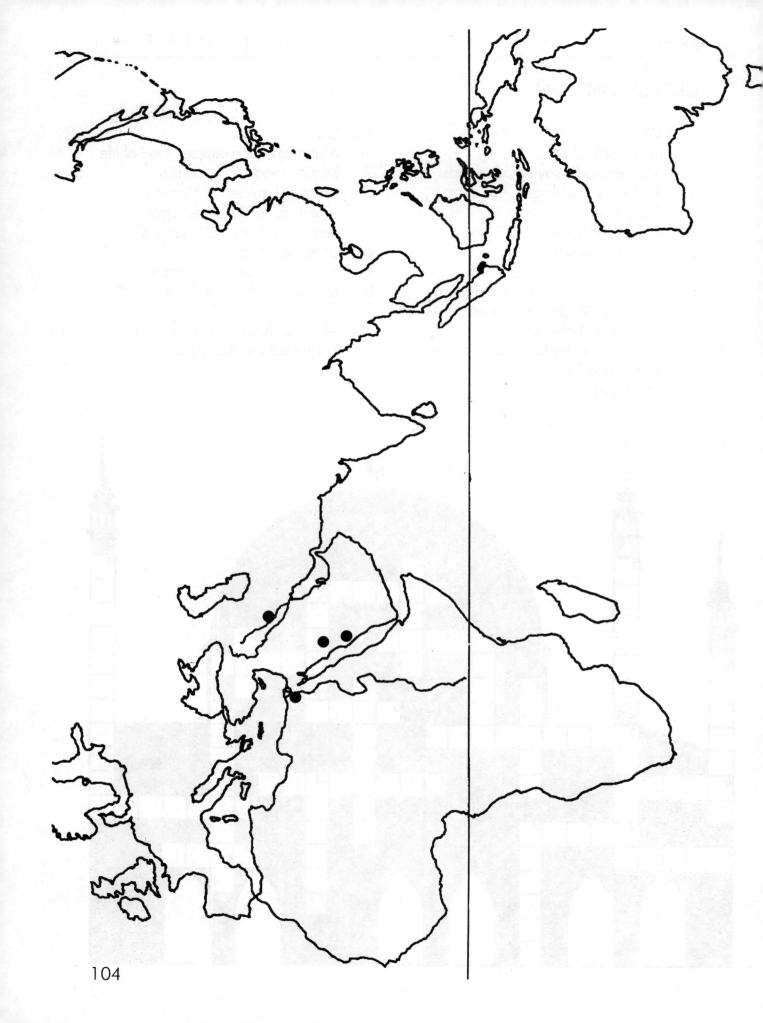

MAP SKILLS

Use the maps in your text to fill in the information on the map facing this page.

1. Label all the continents shown.

2. Draw a line from Yemen to Rome along the ancient trade route.

3. Put a circle around the city where Muhammad was born.

4. Put a box around the city to which the Muslims migrated.
    What was its old name? _____

5. Put a triangle around the city of Baghdad. Label the two rivers near it.

6. Draw two green arrows showing the directions of Islam's spread after Muhammad's death.

7. Label the Nile River. Color the Nile Delta yellow.
    What city did the Muslims found at the bottom of the delta?

    _____

8. Label India and China.

9. Label three oceans and three seas on the map.

10. Draw four blue lines to places where Muslims traded.

WORDS FROM ARABIC

There are many words in the English language which came from Arabic.
Many of these words are names of products from Muslim lands. Others are
scientific words, or terms from navigation and travel. Guess these "English-
Arabic" words from the pictures and fill in the letter spaces with their names.

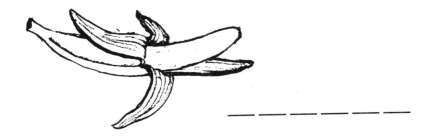

_ _ _ _ _ _

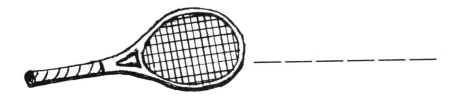

_ _ _ _ _ _

_ _ _ _ _ _

_ _ _ _ _ _

ARABIC NUMERALS

The number signs you use every day are called "Arabic numerals." The idea of using a separate symbol for each number from 1 to 9 was brought by Muslims from India in the 900s. Before these Arabic numerals came to Europe, Roman numerals were used. To find out which symbols are easier to use, practice using them by answering the questions below. By reading the numerals on the clocks below, you can figure out which number is which.

 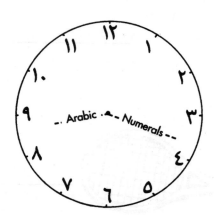

1. Write the symbol for three in Roman _____ and Arabic_____numerals.
2. Write the number twelve in Roman _____ and Arabic _____ numerals.
3. How do you think the number 15 is written?
   in Roman numerals _____   in Arabic numerals_____

The idea of using zero (0) to hold empty places in 10s,100s and so on, was also brought by Muslims from India.

4. Write the number ten in Arabic numerals. _____
   What symbol is used for zero? _____
5. Try writing these numbers in Arabic numerals:
   One hundred _____   Forty-five _____
   Can you do it in Roman numerals?

Modern Arabic numberals, above, are different from those that first came from Arabs. Those were like ours today. Arabic numerals are easy to use in arithmetic problems. Try solving these, using the clock above to help you remember the number which stands for each symbol.

	LXVII		LXXXII		49177		935629
+	CLIX	+	MCCXIV	+	1072311	+	121436
	_____		_____		_____		_____